On
Leading with
Purpose

T0383826

HBR's 10 Must Reads series is the definitive collection of ideas and best practices for aspiring and experienced leaders alike. These books offer essential reading selected from the pages of *Harvard Business Review* on topics critical to the success of every manager.

Titles include:

HBR's 10 Must Reads 2015
HBR's 10 Must Reads 2016
HBR's 10 Must Reads 2017
HBR's 10 Must Reads 2018
HBR's 10 Must Reads 2019
HBR's 10 Must Reads 2020
HBR's 10 Must Reads 2021
HBR's 10 Must Reads 2022
HBR's 10 Must Reads 2023
HBR's 10 Must Reads 2024
HBR's 10 Must Reads 2025
HBR's 10 Must Reads for Business Students
HBR's 10 Must Reads for CEOs
HBR's 10 Must Reads for Executive Teams
HBR's 10 Must Reads for Mid-Level Managers
HBR's 10 Must Reads for New Managers
HBR's 10 Must Reads on AI
HBR's 10 Must Reads on AI, Analytics, and the New Machine Age
HBR's 10 Must Reads on Boards
HBR's 10 Must Reads on Building a Great Culture
HBR's 10 Must Reads on Business Model Innovation
HBR's 10 Must Reads on Career Resilience
HBR's 10 Must Reads on Change Management (Volumes 1 and 2)
HBR's 10 Must Reads on Collaboration
HBR's 10 Must Reads on Communication (Volumes 1 and 2)
HBR's 10 Must Reads on Creativity
HBR's 10 Must Reads on Data Strategy
HBR's 10 Must Reads on Design Thinking
HBR's 10 Must Reads on Diversity
HBR's 10 Must Reads on Emotional Intelligence

HBR's 10 Must Reads on Employee Engagement
HBR's 10 Must Reads on Entrepreneurship and Startups
HBR's 10 Must Reads on High Performance
HBR's 10 Must Reads on Innovation
HBR's 10 Must Reads on Leadership (Volumes 1 and 2)
HBR's 10 Must Reads on Leadership for Healthcare
HBR's 10 Must Reads on Leadership Lessons from Sports
HBR's 10 Must Reads on Leading Digital Transformation
HBR's 10 Must Reads on Leading with Purpose
HBR's 10 Must Reads on Leading Winning Teams
HBR's 10 Must Reads on Lifelong Learning
HBR's 10 Must Reads on Making Smart Decisions
HBR's 10 Must Reads on Managing Across Cultures
HBR's 10 Must Reads on Managing in a Downturn, Expanded Edition
HBR's 10 Must Reads on Managing People (Volumes 1 and 2)
HBR's 10 Must Reads on Managing Projects and Initiatives
HBR's 10 Must Reads on Managing Risk
HBR's 10 Must Reads on Managing Yourself (Volumes 1 and 2)
HBR's 10 Must Reads on Mental Toughness
HBR's 10 Must Reads on Negotiation
HBR's 10 Must Reads on Nonprofits and the Social Sectors
HBR's 10 Must Reads on Organizational Resilience
HBR's 10 Must Reads on Performance Management
HBR's 10 Must Reads on Platforms and Ecosystems
HBR's 10 Must Reads on Public Speaking and Presenting
HBR's 10 Must Reads on Reinventing HR
HBR's 10 Must Reads on Sales
HBR's 10 Must Reads on Strategic Marketing
HBR's 10 Must Reads on Strategy (Volumes 1 and 2)
HBR's 10 Must Reads on Strategy for Healthcare
HBR's 10 Must Reads on Strengthening Your Soft Skills
HBR's 10 Must Reads on Talent
HBR's 10 Must Reads on Teams
HBR's 10 Must Reads on Trust
HBR's 10 Must Reads on Women and Leadership
HBR's 10 Must Reads: The Essentials

On Leading with Purpose

HARVARD BUSINESS REVIEW PRESS
Boston, Massachusetts

Copyright 2025 Harvard Business School Publishing Corporation
All rights reserved
Printed in the United States of America
10 9 8 7 6 5 4 3 2 1

No part of this publication may be reproduced, stored in or introduced into a retrieval system, or transmitted, in any form, or by any means (electronic, mechanical, photocopying, recording, or otherwise), without the prior permission of the publisher. Requests for permission should be directed to permissions@harvardbusiness.org, or mailed to Permissions, Harvard Business School Publishing, 60 Harvard Way, Boston, Massachusetts 02163.

The web addresses referenced in this book were live and correct at the time of the book's publication but may be subject to change.

Cataloging-in-Publication data is forthcoming.

ISBN: 979-8-89279-097-0
eISBN: 979-8-89279-098-7

The paper used in this publication meets the requirements of the American National Standard for Permanence of Paper for Publications and Documents in Libraries and Archives Z39.48-1992.

Contents

BONUS ARTICLE FROM HBR.ORG
Use Storytelling to Explain Your Company's Purpose   177
   by John Coleman

On
Leading with
Purpose

Put Purpose at the Core of Your Strategy

by Thomas W. Malnight, Ivy Buche, and Charles Dhanaraj

EIGHT YEARS AGO we launched a global study of high growth in companies, investigating the importance of three strategies known to drive it: creating new markets, serving broader stakeholder needs, and changing the rules of the game. What we found surprised us. Although each of those approaches did boost growth at the organizations we studied, there was a fourth driver we hadn't considered at all: *purpose*.

Companies have long been encouraged to build purpose into what they do. But usually it's talked about as an add-on—a way to create shared value, improve employee morale and commitment, give back to the community, and help the environment. But as we worked with the high-growth companies in our study and beyond, we began to recognize that many of them had moved purpose from the periphery of their strategy to its core—where, with committed leadership and financial investment, they had used it to generate sustained profitable growth, stay relevant in a rapidly changing world, and deepen ties with their stakeholders.

Two Critical Roles

In the course of our research, we talked to scores of C-level executives. They worked at 28 companies—in the United States, Europe, and India—that had had an average compound annual growth rate of

1

30% or more in the previous five years. What we learned from those conversations was that purpose played two important strategic roles: It helped companies *redefine the playing field*, and it allowed them to *reshape the value proposition*. And that, in turn, enabled them to overcome the challenges of slowing growth and declining profitability.

Role 1: Redefining the playing field

What's a key difference between low-growth and high-growth companies? The former spend most of their time fighting for market share on one playing field, which naturally restricts their growth potential. And because most aggressive battles take place in industries that are slowing down, gains in market share come at a high cost, often eroding profits and competitive advantage as offerings become commoditized.

High-growth companies, by contrast, don't feel limited to their current playing field. Instead, they think about whole ecosystems, where connected interests and relationships among multiple stakeholders create more opportunities. But these firms don't approach ecosystems haphazardly. They let purpose be their guide.

Consider the different strategies adopted by the two leading companies in the pet-food industry: Nestlé Purina PetCare, the largest player in North America; and Mars Petcare, the global leader. The companies have defined very similar purposes for themselves—"Better with pets" (Purina) and "A better world for pets" (Mars Petcare)—and both want to develop new products that will help customers improve their pets' health. But Purina has continued to focus on the pet-food playing field and is applying purpose in some inspiring social initiatives, whereas Mars Petcare is using purpose to propel its expansion in the broader field of pet health.

Mars Petcare, which had established a foothold in pet health with the acquisition of Banfield Pet Hospital in 2007, decided to build its presence in that arena by buying two other veterinary services: BluePearl in 2015 and VCA in 2017. Then in 2018 Mars Petcare entered the European veterinary market, buying the Swedish company AniCura, which has operations in seven European countries, and the British

Idea in Brief

The Challenge

Companies pursuing high growth tend to follow three well-known strategies: creating new markets, serving broader stakeholder needs, and changing the rules of the game. But there's another critical growth driver: purpose.

The Insight

Many companies consider purpose merely an add-on to their strategy, but the most successful companies put it at the core, using it to redefine the playing field and reshape their value propositions.

The Benefits

A purpose-driven strategy helps companies overcome the challenges of slowing growth and declining profits. It also helps with the soft side of management: the people-related aspects of running a business, which so often prove to be the undoing of leaders.

---

company Linnaeus. Those acquisitions helped Mars Petcare become Mars Inc.'s largest and fastest-growing business division.

In moving deeper into this larger ecosystem, Mars Petcare did more than just capitalize on a burgeoning industry. It also shifted its orientation beyond products to services, a radical change for an asset-heavy company that for 75 years had relied on the production and sale of goods. To succeed, the company had to build completely different core competencies and devise a new organizational structure. Many companies in this dangerously open-ended situation might have flailed, but Mars Petcare did not. It was able to pull off a transformation because it ensured that every move it made was aligned with the same core purpose. And it's not done yet: The company is now bringing that sense of purpose to efforts to expand into pet-activity monitoring with "smart" collars.

Another company that has used purpose to redefine the playing field, this time in the industrial sector, is the Finnish oil-refining firm Neste. For more than six decades Neste, founded in 1948, operated a business focused almost entirely on crude oil, but by 2009 it was struggling. The market was glutted, oil prices had dropped sharply, margins were falling, and the EU had passed new carbon-emissions legislation. During the previous two years the company's market value had shrunk by 50%.

Fighting those headwinds, the executive team, led by Neste's new CEO, Matti Lievonen, realized that the company could no longer survive on its traditional playing field. It would have to look for new opportunities in the larger ecosystem. Renewable energy could be a key driver of growth, they realized. Their purpose, they decided, should be to develop sustainable sources of energy that would help reduce emissions, and everything they did would be guided by a simple idea: "Creating responsible choices every day."

It's common for major oil companies to nod to sustainability in some way, but Lievonen quickly proved that Neste meant business, launching a bold transformation that would become a seven-year journey. Employees, customers, and investors all initially resisted the change, but Lievonen and his team were undaunted. They made major investments in infrastructure, innovated renewable technologies, focused on converting customers to green energy solutions, and, most important, engineered a fundamental change in the company's culture.

The process wasn't easy. When Lievonen was just three months into his tenure, a leading economic magazine in Finland published an article saying that he should be fired. He soldiered on, however, and by 2015 Neste had established itself as the world's largest producer of renewable fuels derived from waste and residues. A year later its comparable operating profits from renewables would surpass those of its oil-products business. In 2017 the company took yet another step by actively researching and promoting the use of waste feedstock from new sources such as algae oil, microbial oil, and tall oil pitch.

Role 2: Reshaping the value proposition

When confronted with eroding margins in a rapidly commodifying world, companies often enhance their value propositions by innovating products, services, or business models. That can bring some quick wins, but it's a transactional approach geared toward prevailing in the current arena. Because a purpose-driven approach facilitates growth in new ecosystems, it allows companies to broaden their mission, create a holistic value proposition, and deliver lifetime benefits to customers.

Companies can make this shift in three main ways: by responding to trends, building on trust, and focusing on pain points.

Responding to trends. In line with its purpose of "contributing to a safer society," Sweden's Securitas AB, a security company with 370,000 employees, has traditionally offered physical guarding services. But in the early 2010s its CEO at the time, Alf Göransson, saw that globalization, urbanization, and the increasingly networked business landscape were all changing the nature of risk—for people, operations, and business continuity. At the same time, labor was becoming more expensive, and new technologies were becoming cheaper. Given those developments, Göransson decided that Securitas could no longer "simply sell man-hours." Instead, the company had to explore new ways of using electronics to provide security. This shift, Göransson understood, was not a threat to the existing business but an opportunity to grow—as indeed it has proved to be.

In 2018 the company decided to go a step further and reshape its value proposition from reactive to predictive security, a plan that once again built on the company's core purpose. Under the leadership of Göransson's successor, Magnus Ahlqvist, the firm strengthened its electronic security business by acquiring a number of companies, investing heavily in modernizing and integrating back-office systems, and training its guards in remote surveillance, digital reporting, and efficient response. That allowed Securitas to offer bundled, customized security solutions—encompassing physical guarding, electronic security, and risk management—that provided a much-enhanced level of protection at an optimized cost. By expanding its value proposition in this way, Securitas has been able to strengthen client relationships and significantly increase its margins for the solutions business. From 2012 to 2018 the company's sales of security solutions and electronic security also increased, from 6% of total revenue to 20%.

Building on trust. When Mahindra Finance, the financial services arm of the Mahindra Group, a $20 billion Indian conglomerate, wanted to define its value proposition, it looked to its parent company's longtime purpose-driven strategy of improving customers' lives—encapsulated in 2010 by the simple motto "Rise." It's a word that the company's third-generation leader, Anand Mahindra, expects will inspire employees to accept no limits, think alternatively, and drive positive change.

In keeping with that strategy, Mahindra Finance decided to target its core offering, vehicle financing, to rural areas, where it could—as Rajeev Dubey, the group head of HR, put it to us—"address the unmet needs of underserved customers in an underpenetrated market."

That meant that the company had to figure out how to determine the creditworthiness of customers who were mostly poor, illiterate, and unbanked, with no identity documents, no collateral, and cash flows that were often impacted by monsoons. To do that, the company had to develop completely new ways to handle loan design, repayment terms, customer approval, branch locations, and disbursement and collection in cash. Not only that, but it had to figure out how to recruit workers who could speak local dialects, assess local situations, and operate under a decentralized model of decision-making.

Remarkably, the company managed to do all those things and established a preliminary level of trust with its customers. It then stretched its value proposition to help farmers and other customers obtain insurance for their tractors, lives, and health. In a country where insurance penetration is abysmally low (about 3.5%), this was no small feat, especially since rural residents didn't easily part with any minuscule monthly surplus they had, even if it was to secure their livelihood.

Then Mahindra Finance extended its purpose-driven efforts to housing finance, another arena in which it recognized that it could help its rural customers rise above their circumstances. For most of those people, securing loans for housing was difficult in the extreme. Banks offered loans at an interest rate of about 10% but demanded

Is Purpose at the Core of Your Strategy?

NOT UNLESS you answer yes to all five questions below.

	Y	N
1. Does purpose contribute to increasing your company's growth and profitability today?	❏	❏
2. Does purpose significantly influence your strategic decisions and investment choices?	❏	❏
3. Does purpose shape your core value proposition?	❏	❏
4. Does purpose affect how you build and manage your organizational capabilities?	❏	❏
5. Is purpose on the agenda of your leadership team every time you meet?	❏	❏

documentation most rural residents couldn't provide. Money-lenders offered instant financing but charged interest rates of about 40%. Recognizing an opportunity, Mahindra Finance decided to play at the intermediate level, offering customized home loans at rates of about 14%, an option that appealed to its growing base of customers. And when some of those customers developed successful small agribusinesses, they began looking for working-capital loans, equipment loans, project finance, and so on—more unmet needs that Mahindra Finance could address. So it extended its value proposition again, into the small-to-medium-enterprise arena, offering finance and asset-management services.

Throughout its expansion, Mahindra Finance was guided by its goal of helping rural citizens improve their lives. The company identified and committed itself to value propositions that allowed it to deepen its relationship with its customers, which in turn created additional streams of revenue and profits. Today Mahindra Finance is India's largest rural nonbanking financial company, serving 50% of villages and 6 million customers.

Focusing on pain points. We've already seen how Mars Petcare's health-care value proposition led to direct connections with pet owners at multiple touchpoints. Having established them, the company looked for other ways to create "a better world for pets." How could it come up with a value proposition that would make pet ownership a seamless, convenient, and attractive experience?

The answer was by investing in technology to help address one of the biggest concerns of pet owners: *preventing* health problems. In 2016 the company acquired Whistle, the San Francisco–based maker of a connected collar for activity monitoring and location tracking—a kind of Fitbit for dogs. Teaming the device up with its Banfield Pet Hospital unit, the company launched the Pet Insight Project, a three-year longitudinal study that aims to enroll 200,000 dogs in the United States. By combining machine learning, data science, and deep veterinary expertise, the project seeks to understand when behavior may signal a change in a pet's health and how owners can partner with their veterinarians on individualized diagnostics and treatments for their pets.

Developing a Purpose

Leaders and companies that have effectively defined corporate purpose typically have done so with one of two approaches: *retrospective* or *prospective.*

The retrospective approach builds on a firm's existing reason for being. It requires that you look back, codify organizational and cultural DNA, and make sense of the firm's past. The focus of the discovery process is internal. Where have we come from? How did we get here? What makes us unique to all stakeholders? Where does our DNA open up future opportunities we believe in? These are the kinds of questions leaders have to ask.

Anand Mahindra very successfully employed this tactic at the Mahindra Group. First he looked back at his 30 years at the company and at the values that had guided him as its leader. Then he delved into the psyche of the organization by conducting internal surveys of managers at all levels. He also did ethnographic research in seven countries to identify themes that resonated with his company's multinational, cross-cultural employee base. The process took three years, but ultimately Mahindra arrived at "Rise," which, he realized, had been fundamental to the company from its inception. "'Rise' is not a clever tagline," he has said. "We were already living and operating this way."

The prospective approach, on the other hand, reshapes your reason for being. It requires you to look forward, take stock of the broader ecosystem in which you want to work, and assess your potential for impact in it. The idea is to make sense of the future and then start gearing your organization for it. The focus is external, and leaders have to ask a different set of questions: Where can we go? Which trends affect our business? What new needs, opportunities, and challenges lie ahead? What role can we play that will open up future opportunities for ourselves that we believe in?

The prospective approach can be particularly useful for new CEOs. In 2018, when Magnus Ahlqvist took charge at Securitas, he spearheaded a "purpose workstream" to capture aspirations for the company from the ground up. He asked all his business-unit leaders to run "listening workshops" (with groups of employees from diverse functions, levels, age groups, genders, and backgrounds), which were held over six months. At the end of that period, the findings were collated and analyzed. Among the discoveries: Employees had a vision of transforming the company from a *service provider* to a *trusted adviser*. That shift would require anticipating and responding to security issues instead of relying on the legacy methods of observing and reporting. So employee input helped executives refine the firm's predictive-security strategy.

Implementing a Purpose-Driven Strategy

Our research shows that a compelling purpose clarifies what a company stands for, provides an impetus for action, and is aspirational. But some purpose statements are so generic that they could apply to any company (like Nissan's, "Enriching people's lives"), while others provide only a narrow description of the company's existing businesses (like Wells Fargo's, "We want to satisfy our customers' financial needs and help them succeed financially"). Even if organizations do manage to define their purpose well, they often don't properly translate it into action—or do anything at all to fulfill it. In those cases the purpose becomes nothing more than nice-sounding words on a wall.

Leaders need to think hard about how to make purpose central to their strategy. The two best tactics for doing that are to *transform the leadership agenda* and to *disseminate purpose throughout the organization.*

Consider Mars Petcare again. In 2015 its president, Poul Weihrauch, significantly altered the composition and focus of the leadership team. Its new collective agenda, he declared, would go beyond the performance of individual businesses; it would include generating "multiplier effects" among the businesses (such as between pet food and pet health) and increasing their contributions to creating a better world for pets.

In keeping with that principle, Weihrauch had the company adopt an "outside-in" approach to meeting stakeholder needs. As part of this effort, in 2018 Mars Petcare launched two new programs to support startups innovating in pet care: Leap Venture Studio, a business accelerator formed in partnership with Michelson Found Animals and R/GA; and Companion Fund, a $100 million venture-capital fund in partnership with Digitalis Ventures. In announcing these initiatives the company declared that its ambition was "to become a partner of choice for everyone willing to change the rules of the game in pet care."

Revising a leadership agenda and restructuring an organization are arguably easier at a privately held company like Mars Petcare than at a publicly held one. But Finland's Neste is public, with a major stake held by the government, and it has managed to do both things very effectively.

Neste faced an uphill battle when it decided to move into renewables. The company had to build new capabilities while confronting strong opposition from many employees who didn't buy into the change in direction. About 10% of them left during the first year of the strategy's implementation. Painful as it was, it proved to be a positive development, since the company could not have forged ahead with people who didn't believe in its new purpose.

And forge ahead it did. Neste put in place a new top management team, mobilized its 1,500 R&D engineers, innovated patented renewable technology, and invested €2 billion in building new refineries.

The shift also raised a big question for Neste. How could it change its organizational mindset from *volume* to *value* selling—which entailed convincing customers that its clean fuels would be better for them in the long run? That shift meant going beyond wholesalers to work directly with the distributors and even the distributors' customers. The new leadership team realized that a much higher level of collaboration among business segments and functions was imperative. Winning deals was no longer the sole responsibility of the sales department. The expertise of the whole organization—product knowledge, marketing, finance, taxation—would be required to understand the specific needs of customers like airlines and bus fleets. So Neste engineered a major reorganization and created a matrix structure, in the process rotating about 25% of senior managers and about 50% of upper professionals into new positions. Targets and incentive plans became cross-functional, designed to build capabilities both within and across businesses. And at every step, purpose helped everybody in the company understand the "why" (the business environment's increasing emphasis on sustainability), the "what" (value-creation programs offering renewable solutions to customers, which in turn generated higher margins for Neste), and the "how" (changing from a sales organization to a key-account management model with dedicated people responsible for strategic customers).

The process worked. Neste is now a leader in the renewables industry, and the world is starting to pay attention. In 2015, for example, Google and UPS began partnering with the company to reduce their carbon emissions, as did several cities in California, among them San Francisco and Oakland. In 2018, *Forbes* ranked Neste second on its Global 100 list of the world's most-sustainable companies.

Benefits on the Soft Side

Purpose can also help with the soft side of management—the people-related aspects of running a business, which so often prove to be the undoing of leaders. By putting purpose at the core of strategy, firms can realize three specific benefits: more-unified organizations, more-motivated stakeholders, and a broader positive impact on society.

Unifying the organization

When companies pursue dramatic change and move into larger ecosystems, as both Mars Petcare and Securitas have done, it's unsettling for employees. Why does a pet-food company need to develop a platform to support technology startups? Why does an on-site guarding company want to provide electronic security services that could, over time, make the physical presence of guards redundant? Purpose helps employees understand the whys and get on board with the new direction.

Motivating stakeholders

According to the Edelman Trust Barometer, distrust of government, businesses, the media, and NGOs is now pervasive. At the same time, more than ever, employees, especially Millennials, want to work for organizations that can be trusted to contribute to a higher cause. And when customers, suppliers, and other stakeholders see that a company has a strong higher purpose, they are more likely to trust it and more motivated to interact with it.

Broadening impact

Strategy involves exploring some fundamental questions. Why are we in this business? What value can we bring? What role does my unit play within the bigger portfolio? Purpose creates a basis for answering those questions and defining how each unit will contribute to the organization and to society as a whole. This focus on collective objectives, in turn, opens up many more opportunities to improve growth and profitability today and in the future.

––––––––––––––

The approach to purpose that we're recommending cannot be a one-off effort. Leaders need to constantly assess how purpose can guide strategy, and they need to be willing to adjust or redefine this relationship as conditions change. That demands a new kind of sustained focus, but the advantages it can confer are legion.

Originally published in September–October 2019. Reprint R1905D

What Is the Purpose of Your Purpose?

by Jonathan Knowles, B. Tom Hunsaker, Hannah Grove, and Alison James

TODAY'S BUSINESS LEADERS are under pressure to come up with a corporate purpose, much as they were challenged to develop vision and mission statements in the 1980s and 1990s. Although this focus on the role of corporations in the economy and broader society has many positive aspects, a risk is that speed, shortcuts, and spin may take precedence over authentic action. Our goal in this article is to help executive leaders be clear-sighted about what they seek to define: the purpose of their purpose.

Purpose has become something of a fad and a victim of its own success. Companies are aware that their customers and employees are paying more attention to it as part of a wider reassessment of the role of corporations in society. BlackRock's CEO, Larry Fink, and other major investors are urging executives to articulate a role for their companies beyond profit making, implying that doing so will affect their valuation. But despite its sudden elevation in corporate life, purpose remains a confusing subject of sharply polarized debate. Our research indicates that a primary cause of this confusion is that "purpose" is used in three senses: *competence* ("the function that our product serves"); *culture* ("the intent with which we run our business"); and *cause* ("the social good to which we aspire").

Cause-based purposes tend to receive the most attention, largely because companies that push for societal change are more visible. But any of the three types can be effective when pursued appropriately. A competence-based purpose (such as Mercedes's "First Move the World") expresses a clear value proposition to customers and the employees responsible for delivering on it. A culture-based purpose (such as Zappos's "To Live and Deliver WOW") can create internal alignment and collaboration with key partners. A cause-based purpose (such as Patagonia's "in business to save our home planet" or Tesla's "to accelerate the world's transition to sustainable energy") promotes the idea that it is possible to do well by doing good. All three types can create a meaningful *why*.

For any individual company, determining the purpose of its purpose is fundamentally a business decision and must be anchored in strategy. Finding the right answer involves identifying the most authentic and motivating basis for alignment among the key stakeholder groups on which the success of the business depends. That is easier said than done, because multiple business functions have a vested interest in and a specific perspective on purpose. It sits at the intersection of four business agendas: (1) For marketing and sales, it can help win customers and enhance their loyalty. (2) For HR, it can attract, engage, and retain employees. (3) For governance and sustainability, it can enhance environmental, social, and governance performance. (4) For strategy and finance, it can guide how resources are allocated and risks are managed.

Any exploration of purpose begins with recognizing that these agendas are valid inputs to the process. We four—a former CMO, a former CHRO, a professor of global business, and a strategy consultant—represent each of the main constituencies, and we believe that although every company needs a purpose, not every purpose must take the form of a social cause. Of course every company should work to become a better corporate citizen, through programs that actively address climate change and pollution, workplace safety, diversity, and employee well-being, and invest in local communities. As other scholars have shown, improving ESG performance (especially in areas that are most material in your

Idea in Brief

The Problem

Despite its sudden elevation in corporate life, "purpose" remains a confusing concept. Finding the right one involves identifying an authentic and motivating basis for alignment among key stakeholder groups.

Why It Exists

Purpose is used in three distinct senses: competence, as in "the function that our product serves";

culture, as in "the intent with which we run our business"; and cause, as in "the social good we aspire to."

The Solution

Not all companies can save the world. Only a minority should put forward a cause-based purpose. For the rest, a functionally useful business or a strong culture can provide the basis for a meaningful and motivating *why*.

industry) is good for business. But it is distinct from the *purpose* of a business.

In this article we'll provide three key rules regarding the role of purpose; our observations about what companies typically get wrong about it; and a framework for evaluating which of the three types is likely to be most effective for a company.

1. Don't Rally Around a Cause Unless You Actually Have One

Discussions about purpose typically start with the question, How would the world be worse off if we did not exist? This spurs people to identify an inspiring social impact that the business should strive to achieve. However, only a limited number of companies operate in industries where the nature of the business lends itself to a compelling answer to that question. Examples include Beyond Meat, whose purpose is to find "a better way to feed the planet," and Disney, which aims to "create happiness through magical experiences." Health, science, and clean energy companies fall into this category too. However, focusing on this question too much may lead the majority of companies to misrepresent the actual nature of their business—as WeWork did in its 2019 investor prospectus when it described subletting office space as striving "to elevate the world's consciousness," and Knorr (a brand known for stock cubes and gravy) did when it suggested that consumers could "change the world by changing what's on [their] plate."

Being able to define a social-cause-based North Star may be of benefit primarily to consumer-facing enterprises. But few others—particularly if they're in B2B sectors such as basic materials, energy generation, capital goods, commercial transportation, and business services—have any particular higher purpose to which they can authentically lay claim.

2. A Strong Culture Is Often All You Need

The current fixation on purpose puts pressure on executives to be seen as running a "good" business. Sometimes, however, it's enough simply to run a business well. Culture-based purpose statements are a great option for companies that provide necessary products and services but don't present credibly as agents of positive social change. This is especially true when their success depends on high levels of employee engagement and collaboration with both suppliers and distributors. Those stakeholders are primarily interested in what the company is really like to work for or with rather than in its aspirations to have a broader impact on society.

Defining your purpose as embedded in culture—as operating in a thoughtful, disciplined, ethical manner—can be both pragmatic and genuine. Consider Mars, a family-owned consumer packaged goods company, which in 2019 unveiled its first purpose statement in more than 100 years of operation: "The world we want tomorrow starts with how we do business today." While this expresses aspiration for a better future, its focus is on the "how" of the company's culture—specifically its Five Principles (such as "We base decisions on Mutuality of benefit to our stakeholders" and "We harness the power of Efficiency to use our resources to maximum effect") that since they were first published in 1983, have actively guided the attitudes and behaviors of all Mars associates.

Contrast that with the initial approach to purpose of Mars's rival Nestlé. In 2014 the company began positioning itself as "the world's leading nutrition, health and wellness company"—a descriptor it was forced to retract when commentators observed that nearly three-quarters of its earnings were from snacks and confectionary. The company subsequently retreated to the more believable "Good food, good life."

Choosing culture as the focus of your purpose statement can be a powerful way to attract talent. An engaged workforce is a key business driver. Conversely, Gallup has estimated that the cost of disengagement—in the form of turnover, low productivity, and low morale—can come to about 18% of salary costs.

A focus on culture may take one of three forms, each of which can establish a powerful sense of community and belonging among employees and business partners. Cultural *consistency* stresses

The three senses of purpose

Despite its elevation in corporate life, purpose remains a confusing subject of sharply polarized debate. A primary reason is that it can be understood in three distinct ways.

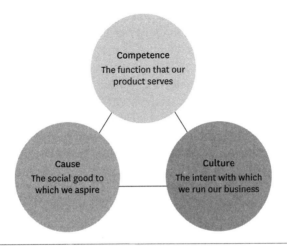

adherence to a code for the business—such as the J&J credo and Mars's Five Principles. Cultural *fit* emphasizes an aspect of the culture that will attract employees and partners who are similarly inclined. Examples include Bridgewater Associates' culture of "radical transparency" and Zappos's belief that great customer service depends on "[getting] the culture right." Cultural *diversity* focuses on promoting inclusiveness and celebrating employees and partners for their differences as much as for their similarities. This approach is particularly effective at companies such as airlines and financial services, whose business models require that their employee base closely match the diversity of their customer base.

3. Don't Delegate Purpose to the Marketing Team Alone

Because CEOs assume that the marketing team is most closely in touch with consumer sentiment, some combination of marketing and corporate communications is often tasked with articulating the corporate purpose. But given that marketing's objective is to generate demand for the company's products and services, the purpose initiative may devolve into an exercise in appealing to consumer preferences. Because research shows that most consumers, and especially Millennials, prefer to buy from companies with a cause-driven purpose, the marketing and corporate communications teams will almost inevitably arrive at an elevated statement that puts the company in a highly flattering light.

At the extreme, conflating marketing and purpose can lead to the sort of posturing whereby BAT (British American Tobacco) and Philip Morris International claim—without any apparent irony—that their purposes are, respectively, to "build a Better Tomorrow" and to "unsmoke the world and create a better future," even if they are simply trying to promote the next generation of their products rather than reduce consumption of an addictive substance. Consider the less egregious but still poorly received attempts by Pepsi and Gillette to position their brands as advocates for important social issues with which they had little previous involvement. The absence of an intuitive connection between Pepsi and the cause of social justice resulted in widespread criticism of its 2017 advertisement featuring Kendall Jenner. A similar reaction greeted Gillette's 2019 brand repositioning, which replaced "the best a man can get" (in use since 1989) with "the best men can be" in a short film that focused on the problem of toxic masculinity. Although this was and is an important social issue, a history of perpetuating male stereotypes through the sponsorship of macho athletes made Gillette an inauthentic advocate.

That's not to say that purpose can't inspire a successful marketing campaign. Contrast those misfires with Dove's campaign for "real beauty," which used normal women as models. The campaign was born out of marketing research revealing that in 2004 only 2% of women around the world would describe themselves as beautiful (the figure had reached only 4% when the research was repeated in 2010). Dove's functional benefits—cleaning and moisturizing—gave rise to an emotional benefit: self-esteem. The campaign aligned nicely with the purpose of Unilever, Dove's parent company: "making sustainable living commonplace" by investing in and improving the lives of its customers and the communities in which it operates. A marketing campaign is most effective when it is the offspring of a corporate purpose rather than the progenitor of one.

Indeed, some companies with strong cause-based purposes don't focus on them in advertising because they recognize the risk of trivializing or overhyping something central and sacred to the organization. Starbucks defines its purpose as "to inspire and nurture the human spirit—one person, one cup, and one neighborhood at a time," but its advertising highlights the quality and novelty of its products. Likewise, JetBlue's advertising largely focuses on what drives ticket sales rather than on its mission "to inspire humanity— both in the air and on the ground."

Companies that can't credibly claim to produce external benefits or to promote a social cause should accept that satisfying the functional and emotional needs of consumers can be a sufficient foundation for a business. Consider soda and snacks. Consuming them is bad for people from a nutritional point of view. But satisfying "sensorial needs" (to borrow from the doublespeak used by BAT in its purpose video) is a legitimate commercial goal, and companies should be content to acknowledge that they aspire to produce the most delicious ice cream or cookies or potato chips or soda. McDonald's is right to define its mission as "to be our customers' favorite place and way to eat and drink." Nordstrom aims simply "to give customers the most compelling shopping experience possible." This is not to say that McDonald's shouldn't take steps to enhance the nutritional value of its menu or to improve the environmental footprint of its suppliers. Doing so could be good for business in the long term if it reduced the risk of consumer or regulatory blowback. But those goals are manifestly not the *purpose* of its business, and any marketing campaign that positions them as such risks derision.

To avoid that risk, business leaders need a clear understanding of how their corporate purpose extends beyond the objectives of their brands and their advertising. A purpose is about the essence of the company. Its goal is to achieve buy-in from a broad range of stakeholders—whereas the function of brands is to persuade consumers to buy the company's products and services.

That distinction was well made by Business Roundtable in 2019 when it described the purpose of a corporation as promoting "an economy that serves all Americans" by meeting the needs of five groups of stakeholders: customers, employees, suppliers, communities, and shareholders. This clearly articulated the need for companies to think beyond the immediate interests of those who provide their funding and to whom they sell.

What Companies Typically Get Wrong About Purpose

The goal of any company is to attract and retain talent, satisfy customers, and conduct business in a manner that secures its license to operate in the eyes of the community and regulators—all while earning an appealing return on capital. Defining your corporate purpose is an opportunity to demonstrate how your company can satisfy those requirements simultaneously. But, as is always the case with strategy, corporate purpose requires clarity about the trade-offs being made and should result in something that is internally coherent.

Many of the challenges that companies encounter with purpose stem from a perceived lack of alignment between how they behave and what they say they stand for. It is tempting to claim being "purpose driven" because of the appeal to employees and consumers—but that works only if you demonstrate authenticity and coherence.

The competence-cause gap

This lack of alignment occurs when the connection between the nature of your business and your espoused cause is not obvious—a danger for even highly successful companies. For instance, a difficulty currently facing the platforms Facebook and Google is that their advertising-driven business models are perceived to be increasingly at odds with their stated missions: "to build community and bring the world closer together" and "to organize the world's information and make it universally accessible and useful," respectively.

The competence-culture gap

This arises when a company is successful at creating value for customers but is less well regarded as an employer, a business partner, or a corporate citizen. Amazon and Walmart have historically enjoyed high levels of customer approval (reflecting their respective commitments to "be Earth's most customer-centric company" and "saving people money so they can live better") while regularly being criticized for their record as employers, their perceived reluctance to recognize workers' rights, and their lack of transparency in the supply chain.

The culture-cause gap

If your company has a clearly stated, cause-related purpose yet your employee engagement scores are low, you have a culture-cause disconnect. This suggests a need for greater focus on culture and behaviors or a reevaluation of your purpose's authenticity as currently defined. That is the challenge the new management at Uber faced in 2018 and the new executive team at Volkswagen is currently facing: how to reinvent a culture that turned a blind eye to toxic behavior (in Uber's case) and illegal behavior (in VW's case).

A Guide to Finding Your Purpose

We recommend a five-step process for ensuring that your corporate purpose fulfills its role as a key element of your strategy.

1. Identify the internal constituencies that have a stake in your purpose

At most companies the leaders of multiple business functions will want to see that their interests are adequately considered. We've identified four main kinds of interests and their constituencies: *demand generation* (sales, marketing, channel management), *employee engagement* (HR, employee networks), *governance and sustainability* (legal, operations, corporate communications, investor relations, community relations), and *strategy and business valuation* (the CEO, the CFO, risk management). The first step in drafting a purpose is to establish a working team with representatives from each of these constituencies.

2. Remember that purpose can be defined in three ways

The working team's initial discussion should establish a common language around purpose and explore the various ways in which each of its three domains—competence, culture, and cause—is relevant to each of the constituencies represented. How might a culture-based purpose be articulated with the interests of communities in mind? Or a cause-based purpose with the interests of investors in mind? These discussions should take as expansive a view as possible of the range of options for defining corporate purpose, making authenticity the binding constraint.

This approach acknowledges that each type of purpose has advantages. A competence-focused purpose presents a clear value proposition for both customers and employees. A culture-focused purpose creates internal alignment and collaboration with key partners. A cause-focused purpose aligns customers, employees, and communities around the societal benefits that the company generates. There will be points of overlap with the ESG agenda, but the

Where Purpose Affects Your Organization

PURPOSE CAN HAVE AN IMPACT on four business agendas. To determine what that is, ask yourself these questions.

- **Demand generation.** How can purpose increase consumers' preference for our products and services?
- **Employee engagement.** How can purpose strengthen the connection that employees feel to the work and to one another?
- **Governance and sustainability.** How can purpose help reinforce our reputation as a good corporate citizen and a strong ESG performer?
- **Strategy and business valuation.** How can purpose enhance our opportunities for profitable growth and reduce business risk?

purpose effort should go further than simply seeking to address negative external effects.

3. Link purpose to strategy

The third step is to view all the possible ideas for purpose in light of the factors that will have the greatest impact on the company's success over the next decade. Is the key business driver talent acquisition and retention—or is it product innovation? The ability to sustain a premium price? International expansion?

The point is to develop a clear sense of the business objective that the purpose will support. How can it enhance the relevance and sustainability of your value proposition to customers and other stakeholders and strengthen the company's relative advantage? This step typically produces a short list of three to five key ideas for defining your purpose in a way that aligns strongly with the strategy of the business.

4. Transcend siloed thinking

At this point the working team needs to recognize that purpose cannot be authentic if it is motivated only by self-interest and opportunism. The next step is to find an idea that acknowledges but transcends the vested interest of each constituency. The following questions can help in reaching a consensus on the most effective definition of the company's purpose.

- *Is the usefulness of what we provide so self-evident that we need say nothing more?* If so, then a competence-based purpose such as Apple's "bringing the best user experience to its customers through its innovative hardware, software, and services" might be a good fit.

- *Does the nature of our business make it credible for us to assert that we're out to do good?* If, for example, the focus of your business is improving health, then either a cause-based purpose (such as Roche's "doing now what patients need next") or a competence-based one is probably best.

- *Does our leaders' behavior support the idea that we're in the business to make the world a better place, even if that's not our core focus?* A fervent CEO and a cause-based purpose can confer a halo on what is otherwise a rather mundane business. The Salesforce CEO Marc Benioff's public activism on social issues has undoubtedly given credence to the company's claim that its CRM services are intended to "unify people to help business and communities pursue their loftiest goals." The Patagonia founder Yvon Chouinard's values and leadership make the clothing company's assertion that it is "in business to save our home planet" credible.

- *Do we deliver value to customers while also being an attractive employer, partner, and corporate citizen?* If so, then a culture-based purpose might be most appropriate. Zachry Group, a provider of engineering, procurement, and construction services, focuses its purpose on what it wants to be ("a principle-based enterprise that combines the best in people and technology to create a special business experience, seeking always to make a difference") rather than what it actually *does* (design and build industrial facilities). (Disclosure: One of us, Jonathan, has had a paid advisory relationship with Zachry Group in the past.)

- *Does how we do business create value for society in ways unusual for our industry?* Companies that make their IP open source (as Allbirds did with the technology for creating shoe soles that require no hydrocarbons) or that offer "You buy one, we donate one," as Warby Parker does, enjoy significant credibility when positioning themselves as "leading the way for socially conscious business," in the words of the eyewear manufacturer.

We recommend that during deliberations each member of the working team have discussions with other stakeholders—employees, suppliers, business partners, community leaders—to get their input on the ideas under consideration. That will help ensure that the eventual purpose statement is authentic, relevant, and practical.

5. Embed purpose in behavior

The final step of the process is without doubt the hardest—as anyone who has been involved in change management will attest. New modes of behavior that bring a purpose to life need to be modeled by senior leaders and reflected in performance reviews and promotions, recruitment, business decisions, and the culture more broadly.

It is important to recognize that only executives experience purpose as a top-down phenomenon. Most other stakeholders experience it from the bottom up—through their interactions with products and services, employees, physical locations, and communications. From a top-down perspective, it seems logical to begin an exploration of corporate purpose by asking, How would the world be worse off if we did not exist? But from a bottom-up perspective, it is more important that purpose increase the sense of authenticity, coherence, and engagement derived from the day-to-day experiences of customers, employees, partners, and the communities in which the company operates. The ultimate test of your purpose is whether it improves the way the business actually operates.

_____

This decade promises to be remembered as the era of stakeholder capitalism, corporate purpose, and the business lexicon's adoption of the terms "empathy," "equity," "diversity," and "inclusion." We suggest two further important elements: *pragmatism* and *authenticity*.

The full potential of purpose is achieved only when it's aligned with a company's value proposition and creates shared aspirations both internally and externally. At its best, it's the most powerful mechanism for generating buy-in across stakeholders. If enacted poorly or manipulatively, it produces the opposite effect. With so much at stake, getting your purpose right should be one of your most pressing decisions.

Originally published in March–April 2022. Reprint S22021

Creating a Purpose-Driven Organization

by Robert E. Quinn and Anjan V. Thakor

WHEN GERRY ANDERSON FIRST became the president of DTE Energy, he did not believe in the power of higher organizational purpose.

We're not talking about having a clear mission that focuses largely on how a business will generate economic value. DTE had one that set out the goal of creating long-term gains for shareholders, and Anderson understood its importance.

A higher purpose is not about economic exchanges. It reflects something more aspirational. It explains how the people involved with an organization are making a difference, gives them a sense of meaning, and draws their support. But like many of the leaders we've interviewed in our research, Anderson started his tenure as president skeptical about how much it mattered. The concept of higher purpose didn't fit into his mostly economic understanding of the firm.

But then the Great Recession of 2008 hit, and he knew he had to get his people to devote more of themselves to work. Even before the financial crisis, surveys had demonstrated that DTE employees were not very engaged. It was a classic quandary: Employees couldn't seem to break free of old, tired behaviors. They weren't bringing their smarts and creativity to their jobs. They weren't performing up to their potential. Anderson knew that he needed a more committed workforce but did not know how to get one.

That was when retired army major general Joe Robles, then the CEO of USAA and a DTE board member, invited Anderson to visit some USAA call centers. Familiar with the culture of most call centers, Anderson expected to see people going through the motions. Instead he watched positive, fully engaged employees collaborate and go the extra mile for customers. When Anderson asked how this could be, Robles answered that a leader's most important job is "to connect the people to their purpose."

At USAA, he explained, every employee underwent an immersive four-day cultural orientation and made a promise to provide extraordinary service to people who had done the same for their country—members of the military and their families. That training was no small investment, since the company had more than 20,000 employees. Its lessons were continually reinforced through town hall meetings and other forums where people at all levels asked questions and shared ideas about how to fulfill their purpose.

Before the recession, Anderson would have rejected Robles's statement about purpose as empty, simplistic rhetoric. But having run into a dead end in figuring out how to make his own organization thrive, Anderson was reexamining some of his basic assumptions about management, and he was open to what Robles was saying.

When Anderson returned to DTE's Detroit headquarters, he made a video that articulated his employees' higher purpose. (He got that idea from Robles, too.) It showed DTE's truck drivers, plant operators, corporate leaders, and many others on the job and described the impact of their work on the well-being of the community—the factory workers, teachers, and doctors who needed the energy DTE generated. The first group of professional employees to see the video gave it a standing ovation. When union members viewed it, some were moved to tears. Never before had their work been framed as a meaningful contribution to the greater good. The video brought to life DTE's new statement of purpose: "We serve with our energy, the lifeblood of communities and the engine of progress."

What happened next was even more important: The company's leaders dedicated themselves to supporting that purpose and wove

Idea in Brief

The Problem

You've surely seen this happen more than once: Employees get stuck in a rut, disengage from their work, and stop performing to their potential. So managers respond with tighter oversight and control, yet nothing improves.

The Reason

Most management practices and incentives are based on conventional economic logic, which assumes that employees are self-interested agents. And that assumption becomes a self-fulfilling prophecy.

The Solution

By connecting people with a sense of higher purpose, leaders can inspire them to bring more energy and creativity to their jobs. When employees feel that their work has meaning, they become more committed and engaged. They take risks, learn, and raise their game.

it into onboarding and training programs, corporate meetings, and culture-building activities such as film festivals and sing-alongs. As people judged the purpose to be authentic, a transformation began to take place. Engagement scores climbed. The company received a Gallup Great Workplace Award for five years in a row. And financial performance responded in kind: DTE's stock price more than tripled from the end of 2008 to the end of 2017.

Why did purpose work so well after other interventions had failed? Anderson had previously tried to shake things up by providing training, altering incentives, and increasing managerial oversight, with disappointing results. It turned out that his approach was to blame—not his people.

That's a hard truth to recognize. If, like many executives, you're applying conventional economic logic, you view your employees as self-interested agents and design your organizational practices and culture accordingly, and that hasn't paid off as you'd hoped.

So you now face a choice: You can double down on that approach, on the assumption that you just need more or stricter controls to achieve the desired impact. Or you can align the organization with an authentic higher purpose that intersects with your business interests and helps guide your decisions. If you succeed in doing the latter, your people will try new things, move into deep learning, take risks, and make surprising contributions.

Many executives avoid working on their firms' purpose. Why? Because it defies what they have learned in business school and, perhaps, in subsequent experience: that work is fundamentally contractual, and employees will seek to minimize personal costs and effort.

Those are not necessarily faulty assumptions—indeed, they describe the behavior in many environments reasonably well. However, they also amount to a self-fulfilling prophecy. When managers view employees this way, they create the very problems they expect. Employees choose to respond primarily to the incentives outlined in their contracts and the controls imposed on them. Consequently, they not only fail to see opportunities but also experience conflict, resist feedback, underperform, and personally stagnate. So managers, believing that their assumptions about employees have been validated, exert still more control and rely even more heavily on extrinsic incentives. Employees then narrowly focus on achieving those rewards, typically at the expense of activities that are hard to measure and often ignored, such as mentoring subordinates and sharing best practices. Overarching values and goals become empty words. People do only what they have to do. Results again fall short of expectations, and managers clamp down further.

In this article we provide a framework that can help managers break out of this vicious cycle. In our consulting work with hundreds of organizations and in our research—which includes extensive interviews with dozens of leaders and the development of a theoretical model—we have come to see that when an authentic purpose permeates business strategy and decision-making, the personal good and the collective good become one. Positive peer pressure kicks in, and employees are reenergized. Collaboration increases, learning accelerates, and performance climbs. We'll look at how you can set off a similar chain of events in your organization, drawing on examples from a range of companies.

How to Do It

When organizations embrace purpose, it's often because a crisis forces leaders to challenge their assumptions about motivation and performance and to experiment with new approaches. But you don't need to wait for a dire situation. The framework we've developed can help you build a purpose-driven organization when you're *not* backed into a corner. It enables you to overcome the largest barrier to embracing purpose—the cynical "transactional" view of employee motivation—by following eight essential steps.

1. Envision an inspired workforce

According to economists, every employer faces the "principal-agent problem," which is the standard economic model for describing an organization's relationships with its workers. Here's the basic idea: The principal (the employer) and the agent (the employee) form a work contract. The agent is effort-averse. For a certain amount of money, he or she will deliver a certain amount of labor, and no more. Since effort is personally costly, the agent underperforms in providing it unless the principal puts contractual incentives and control systems in place to counter that tendency.

This model precludes the notion of a fully engaged workforce. According to its logic, what Anderson saw at USAA is not possible; it would be foolish to aspire to such an outcome.

One way to change that perception is to expose leaders to positive exceptions to the rule. Consider this July 2015 blog post by Mike Rowe, host of the Discovery Channel show *Dirty Jobs,* about an experience he had at a Hampton Inn:

> I left my hotel room this morning to jump out of a perfectly good airplane, and saw part of a man standing in the hallway. His feet were on a ladder. The rest of him was somewhere in the ceiling.
>
> I introduced myself, and asked what he was doing. Along with satisfying my natural curiosity, it seemed a good way to delay my appointment with gravity, which I was in no hurry to keep. His name is Corey Mundle. . . . We quickly got to talking.

"Well, Mike, here's the problem," he said. "My pipe has a crack in it, and now my hot water is leaking into my laundry room. I've got to turn off my water, replace my old pipe, and get my new one installed before my customers notice there's a problem."

I asked if he needed a hand, and he told me the job wasn't dirty enough. We laughed, and Corey asked if he could have a quick photo. I said sure, assuming he'd return the favor. He asked why I wanted a photo of him, and I said it was because I liked his choice of pronouns.

"I like the way you talk about your work," I said. "It's not 'the' hot water, it's 'MY' hot water. It's not 'the' laundry room, it's 'MY' laundry room. It's not 'a' new pipe, it's 'MY' new pipe. Most people don't talk like that about their work. Most people don't own it."

Corey shrugged and said, "This is not 'a' job; this is 'MY' job. I'm glad to have it, and I take pride in everything I do."

He didn't know it, but Corey's words made my job a little easier that day. Because three hours later, when I was trying to work up the courage to leap out of a perfectly good airplane, I wasn't thinking about pulling the ripcord on the parachute— I was thinking about pulling MY ripcord. On MY parachute.

Corey Mundle is a purpose-driven employee. Instead of minimizing effort as a typical "agent" would, he takes ownership. The fact that people like him exist is important. When coaching executives on how to do purpose work in their organizations, we often tell them, "If it is real, it is possible." If you can find one positive example—a person, a team, a unit that exceeds the norms—you can inspire others. Look for excellence, examine the purpose that drives the excellence, and then imagine it imbuing your entire workforce.

2. Discover the purpose

At a global oil company, we once met with members of a task force asked by the CEO to work on defining the organization's purpose. They handed us a document representing months of work; it articulated a purpose, a mission, and a set of values. We told them it had no power—their analysis and debate had produced only platitudes.

The members of the task force had used only their heads to invent a higher purpose intended to capture employees' hearts. But you do not invent a higher purpose; it already exists. You can discover it through empathy—by feeling and understanding the deepest common needs of your workforce. That involves asking provocative questions, listening, and reflecting.

Deborah Ball, a former dean of the School of Education at the University of Michigan, provides a good example. Like most companies, professional schools experience "mission drift." As a new dean, Ball wanted to clarify her organization's purpose so that she could increase employees' focus, commitment, and collaboration.

To "learn and unlearn the organization," as she put it, she interviewed every faculty member. She expected to find much diversity of opinion—and she did. But she also found surprising commonality, what she called "an emerging story" about the faculty's strong desire to have a positive impact on society. Ball wrote up what she heard and shared it with the people she interviewed. She listened to their reactions and continued to refine their story.

This was not just a listening tour. It was an extended, disciplined, iterative process. Ball says, "You identify gold nuggets, work with them, clarify them, integrate them, and continually feed them back." She refers to the process as "collective creation," borrowing a phrase from agile and design-thinking methodologies.

As that work continued, it became clear that the school had strengths it could use for social good. For example, it had the capacity to influence how other institutions around the world trained teachers, addressed issues of educational affordability, and served underrepresented populations. Ball concluded that these foci had the greatest potential to integrate faculty members' efforts, draw impressive new hires, and attract funding for research. So she highlighted them as crucial elements of the school's collective identity.

3. Recognize the need for authenticity

Purpose has become a popular topic. Even leaders who don't believe in it face pressure from board members, investors, employees, and other stakeholders to articulate a higher purpose. This sometimes leads to statements like the one produced by the task force at the oil company. When a company announces its purpose and values but the words don't govern the behavior of senior leadership, they ring hollow. Everyone recognizes the hypocrisy, and employees become more cynical. The process does harm.

Some CEOs intuitively understand this danger. One actually told his senior leadership team that he didn't want to do purpose work, because organizations are political systems and hypocrisy is inevitable. His statement illustrates an important point: The assumption that people act only out of self-interest also gets applied to leaders, who are often seen as disingenuous if they claim other motivations.

A member of the team responded, "Why don't we change that? Let's identify a purpose and a set of values, and live them with integrity." That earnest comment punctured the existing skepticism, and the team moved ahead.

For an illustration of a purpose that does shape behavior, let's look at Sandler O'Neill and Partners, a midsize investment bank that helps financial institutions raise capital. The company was successful in its niche and focused on the usual goal of maximizing shareholder value. However, on September 11, 2001, disaster struck. Located in the Twin Towers in New York, the company felt the full brunt of the terrorist attack. Jimmy Dunne, soon to lead the firm's executive team, learned that over one-third of Sandler's people, including its top two executives, were dead, and the company's physical infrastructure was devastated. Many of its computers and customer records were gone.

As the crisis unfolded, despite the exceptionally heavy demands of attending to business, Dunne made the decision that a Sandler partner would attend the funeral of every fallen employee, which meant that he attended many funerals. As a result of witnessing so much suffering, he began to realize that the purpose of his firm was not only to satisfy customers and create shareholder value but also to treat employees like valued human beings.

That led to some sharp departures from protocol. For example, he asked his CFO to pay the families of all the dead employees their salaries and bonuses through December 31, 2001—and then asked if the company could do the same for all of 2002. The CFO said the firm could survive, but doing this would be inconsistent with its fiduciary responsibility to the partners. So the firm offered to buy out the ownership stake of any partner at par. Not one accepted.

If your purpose is authentic, people know, because it drives every decision and you do things other companies would not, like paying the families of dead employees. Dunne told us that often an organization discovers its purpose and values when things are going badly—and that its true nature is revealed by what its leaders do in difficult times. He said, "You judge people not by how much they give but by how much they have left after they give."

4. Turn the authentic message into a constant message
When we spoke with the CEO of a global professional services company about how to build a purpose-driven organization, his first question was "When will I be done?"

We responded by telling a story about another CEO, who had been trying to transform his construction company for a year. He showed us his plan and asked our opinion. We told him he deserved an A–. Why wasn't it an A? After giving speeches for a year, he thought he was finished—but his people were just beginning to hear his message. He needed to keep clarifying the organization's purpose for as long as he was CEO. When we told him that, he sank into his chair.

In contrast, Tony Meola, the recently retired head of U.S. consumer operations at Bank of America, is a leader who understands the ongoing nature of purpose work. He says one thing that makes it relentlessly difficult is that it involves getting institutions to shift direction—and existing cultures tend to impede movement. As extensions of the culture, managers, too, end up resisting the change. Other impediments are organizational complexity and competing demands.

Meola overcame those obstacles by clarifying the purpose of his division: treating operational excellence as a destination and allowing no other pressures to distract from it. He emphasized operational skills and leadership in employee training and development, and he brought that focus to every conversation, every decision, every problem his team faced, always asking, "Will this make us better operators?" He says, "When you hold it constant like that, when you never waver, an amazing thing happens. The purpose sinks into the collective conscience. The culture changes, and the organization begins to perform at a higher level. Processes become simpler and easier to execute and sustain. People start looking for permanent solutions rather than stopgap measures that create more inefficiencies through process variations."

Embracing this mindset meant saying no to anything that didn't reflect it. In the division's call center, for example, there had been a proposal to invest additional resources in technology and people so that the group could solve customers' problems faster and better. But the project was rejected because when managers and employees used their stated purpose as a filter and asked themselves whether that investment would make them better operators, the answer was no. What the company really needed to do, they determined, was examine how the operations themselves could be improved to eliminate failures that produced call center inquiries in the first place.

When a leader communicates the purpose with authenticity and constancy, as Meola did, employees recognize his or her commitment, begin to believe in the purpose themselves, and reorient. The change is signaled from the top, and then it unfolds from the bottom.

5. Stimulate individual learning

Conventional economic logic tends to rely on external motivators. As leaders embrace higher purpose, however, they recognize that learning and development are powerful incentives. Employees actually want to think, learn, and grow.

At the St. Louis–based not-for-profit The Mission Continues, whose purpose is to rehabilitate and reintegrate into society wounded and disabled war veterans, new hires are assigned a large amount of work. The underlying philosophy is that when a leader gives someone a difficult challenge, it shows faith in that person's potential. The job becomes an incubator for learning and development, and along the way the employee gains confidence and becomes more committed to the organization and the higher purpose that drives it.

By helping employees understand the relationship between the higher purpose and the learning process, leaders can strengthen it. People at The Mission Continues are required to reflect on that relationship often. Every two weeks they produce a written document describing their purpose, their strengths, and their development. The exercise is not repetitive, because the experiences change, as do the lessons learned. This practice is consistent with research on effective leadership development approaches. In modern organizations, new experiences tend to come easily, but reflection does not.

At The Mission Continues, the employees have become adaptive and proactive. There is less need for managerial control, because they know the purpose and see how it has changed them for the better. You can liken this clear sense of direction to "commander's intent" in the military. If soldiers know and internalize a commander's strategic purpose, they can carry out the mission even when the commander isn't there. This means, of course, that the leader must communicate the organization's higher purpose with utter clarity so that employees can make use of their local information and take initiative. Research by business school professors Claudine Gartenberg, Andrea Prat, and George Serafeim shows how critical this is in corporations, too—it is not unique to nonprofits.

6. Turn midlevel managers into purpose-driven leaders

To build an inspired, committed workforce, you'll need middle managers who not only know the organization's purpose but also deeply connect with it and lead with moral power. That goes way beyond what most companies ask of their midlevel people.

Consider KPMG, a Big Four accounting cooperative with thousands of partners. For decades those partners approached leadership like accounting. They were careful in their observations, exact in their assessments, and cautious about their decisions, because that was the cultural tone set at the top. Senior leaders were not inclined to get emotional about ideals, and neither were the partners. As a result, employees at all levels tended to make only safe, incremental improvements.

But then KPMG went through a transformation. The company began to explore the notion of purpose. Searching its history, its leaders were surprised to find that it had made many significant contributions to major world events. After conducting and analyzing hundreds of employee interviews, they concluded that KPMG's purpose was to help clients "inspire confidence and empower change."

These five words evoked a sense of awe in the firm, but KPMG's top executives avoided the temptation to turn them into a marketing slogan. Instead, they set out to connect every leader and manager to the purpose. They began by talking openly about their own sense of purpose and meaning. When this had an impact, they recognized that the partners needed to do the same with their teams. When senior management shared these expectations, the partners were open to them but did not feel equipped to meet them. So the accounting firm invested in a new kind of training, in which the partners learned how to tell compelling stories that conveyed their sense of personal identity and professional purpose.

Though applying that training was difficult—it was a real stretch for experts in investment, real estate, tax, risk consulting, and so on—the culture did change. Today the partners communicate their personal purpose to their teams and discuss how it links to their professional lives and the organization's reason for being. In doing so, they are modeling a vulnerability and authenticity that no one had previously expected to see at the middle levels of this accounting firm.

7. Connect the people to the purpose

Once leaders at the top and in the middle have internalized the organization's purpose, they must help frontline employees see how it connects with their day-to-day tasks. But a top-down mandate does not work. Employees need to help drive this process, because then the purpose is more likely to permeate the culture, shaping behavior even when managers aren't right there to watch how people are handling things. Our best illustration again comes from KPMG, where employees were encouraged to share their own accounts of how they were making a difference. This evolved into a remarkable program called the 10,000 Stories Challenge. It gave employees access to a user-friendly design program and invited them to create posters that would answer the question "What do you do at KPMG?" while capturing their passion and connecting it to the organization's purpose.

Each participating employee created a purpose-driven headline, such as "I Combat Terrorism," and under it wrote a clarifying statement, such as "KPMG helps scores of financial institutions prevent money laundering, keeping financial resources out of the hands of terrorists and criminals." Beneath the statement, the employee would insert his or her picture. Each poster carried the tagline "Inspire Confidence. Empower Change."

In June company leaders announced that if the staff could create 10,000 posters by Thanksgiving, two extra days would be added to the holiday break. Employees hit that benchmark within a month. But then the process went viral—after the reward had already been earned. Twenty-seven thousand people produced 42,000 posters (some individuals made multiple submissions, and teams produced them as well). KPMG had found a brilliant way to help employees personally identify with its collective purpose.

Once the firm's overall transformation had taken root, surveys showed that employees' pride in their work had increased, and engagement scores reached record levels. The firm eventually climbed 31 places, to the number 12 spot, on *Fortune*'s 100 Best Companies to Work For list, making it the highest ranked of the Big Four. Recruiting improved, and as turnover decreased, costs dropped.

8. Unleash the positive energizers

Every organization has a pool of change agents that usually goes untapped. We refer to this pool as the network of positive energizers. Spread randomly throughout the organization are mature, purpose-driven people with an optimistic orientation, people like Corey Mundle at Hampton Inn. They naturally inspire others. They're open and willing to take initiative. Once enlisted, they can assist with every step of the cultural change. These people are easy to identify, and others trust them.

We have helped launch such networks in numerous organizations, including Prudential Retirement, Kelly Services, and DTE

Energy. Typically, at an initial meeting, senior leaders invite network members to become involved in the design and execution of the change process. Within minutes, there is buy-in. Regular meetings are scheduled. The energizers go out, share ideas, and return with feedback and new ideas. They're willing to tell the truth and openly challenge assumptions.

There is often another benefit, as the experience of one human resources director illustrates. After establishing a network of positive energizers in a major professional services firm, she called us to report that she felt overwhelmed—in a good way—by the interest and commitment of the people she had assembled. They were an amazing resource that, until now, had gone completely unrecognized. They cared as deeply as she did about the organization's purpose and getting colleagues to embrace it. She said, "I no longer feel alone."

Although a higher purpose does not guarantee economic benefits, we have seen impressive results in many organizations. And other research—particularly the Gartenberg study, which included 500,000 people across 429 firms and involved 917 firm-year observations from 2006 to 2011—suggests a positive impact on both operating financial performance (return on assets) and forward-looking measures of performance (Tobin's Q and stock returns) when the purpose is communicated with clarity.

So purpose is not just a lofty ideal; it has practical implications for your company's financial health and competitiveness. People who find meaning in their work don't hoard their energy and dedication. They give them freely, defying conventional economic assumptions about self-interest. They grow rather than stagnate. They do more—and they do it better.

By tapping into that power, you can transform an entire organization.

Originally published in July–August 2018. Reprint R1804E

How Customers Can Rally Your Troops

by Adam M. Grant

HOW DID A FIVE-MINUTE MEETING MOTIVATE university fundraisers to increase their weekly productivity by 400%? How did a photograph drive radiologists to improve the accuracy of their diagnostic findings by 46%?

Was it managers who inspired such enormous results? Perhaps they gave an amazing speech or set clearer goals or tracked performance more carefully. In fact, in both situations, managers were not the catalysts. They did not assume that they alone had to bear the burden of motivating employees with inspiring messages. Instead, they tapped in to a powerful force that encouraged workers to go the extra mile. They *outsourced inspiration* to those who were better suited to the job.

A growing body of research shows that end users—customers, clients, patients, and others who benefit from a company's products and services—are surprisingly effective in motivating people to work harder, smarter, and more productively. A brief visit from a student who had received a scholarship motivated the fundraisers to increase their efforts. A photograph of a patient they had never met inspired the radiologists to read X-rays more accurately. By serving as tangible proof of the consequences and value of employees' efforts, end users such as these can be important allies for leaders in motivating and inspiring their workforces.

Outsourcing inspiration to end users focuses employees' attention squarely on the ultimate impact of their products and services. At Wells Fargo, for instance, managers show bankers videos of people describing how low-interest loans rescued them from severe debt—a vivid reminder to the bankers that they are striving to serve their customers, not their managers. But the power of end users goes beyond their ability to put a name and a face to employees' efforts. Organizational psychologist David Hofmann and I have found that employees generally see end users as more credible than leaders as sources of inspiration. When leaders attempt to deliver inspiring messages, many employees react with skepticism, questioning whether leaders are just trying to get them to work harder. Indeed, researchers Phil Mirvis and Donald Kanter have found that in many companies, the majority of frontline employees are cynical about leaders' motives and intentions. End users, however, can deliver convincing testimonials of their experiences with the company's products and services, showing that leaders' messages are more than rhetoric. Outsourcing inspiration to end users can also keep the content fresh: Leaders can call on multiple customers to deliver distinct messages.

For these reasons, leaders should abandon the notion—popularized in the mainstream business press—of themselves as lone heroes who must rally their employees to do great things. Leaders need help bringing their visions to life, and end users are uniquely suited to this task. In this article, I show how leaders can take full advantage of opportunities for connecting employees to the people affected by their work. Outsourcing inspiration is not about eliminating leaders from the picture; it's about creating a partnership that can enhance the meaning employees derive from their jobs and move them to do their best work.

Employees Without a Cause

The most powerful evidence I've gathered that connecting employees with end users yields motivational benefits comes from a series of experiments with university fundraising callers. These callers,

Idea in Brief

Leaders who connect employees with end users motivate higher performance, measured in terms of revenue as well as supervisors' ratings. Research shows that when leaders are the sole source of inspiring messages, employees often question whether the messages are true. End users, in contrast, are seen as credible sources who can deliver convincing testimonials of their experiences with a company's offerings.

Customers, clients, patients, and others who benefit from a company's products and services

motivate employees by serving as tangible proof of the impact of their work, expressing appreciation for their contributions, and eliciting empathy, which helps employees develop a deeper understanding of customers' needs.

Leaders can "outsource inspiration" to end users (both past and present) by collecting their stories, inviting them to the organization, introducing them to employees, and recognizing employees who make a difference in customers' lives.

whose sole responsibility is to convince alumni to donate money, face motivational challenges common in many sales and service jobs: repetitive work, low autonomy, and rude customers. A large portion of the donated money is used to fund scholarships, but the callers don't see or meet the recipients. One caller had posted a telling sign on his wall: "Doing a good job here is like wetting your pants in a dark suit. You get a warm feeling, but no one else notices." Annual turnover rates in this field can exceed 400%: In a typical three-month period, the entire staff quits, creating exorbitant hiring and training costs.

As part of my research, I have invited several thousand executives to propose ways to motivate the callers to increase their efforts to bring in donations. Most executives start from the assumption that employees are ultimately self-interested, proposing performance incentives such as pay increases, promotions, recognition, food, and breaks—interventions that the fundraising managers had already tried, to no avail.

Rarely do executives suggest imbuing the work with greater meaning and purpose. In fact, fewer than 1% say that managers should show the callers how their work makes a difference. This is consistent with the attitudes of the managers themselves: They give the callers no information about how the donations are used or who benefits from them. Like the executives, they assume the callers are driven by self-interest and simply don't care.

But there's a wealth of evidence that people want to do meaningful work: In national surveys over the past three decades, the vast majority of Americans have identified meaningful work as the single most important feature that they seek in a job. And numerous researchers have found that people are concerned not only about themselves but also about doing work that benefits others and contributes to society.

Once they are armed with this knowledge, executives often suggest that managers deliver inspiring speeches about how the donations are used. But are such messages more powerful coming from a person who benefited from the donations? To test this idea, I invited one scholarship recipient to visit a group of fundraisers who worked in an office filled only with telephones and fellow callers. The student spent five minutes describing how the callers' work had funded his scholarship, how it had made a difference in his life, and how much he appreciated their effort. One month after this visit, the callers showed average increases of 142% in weekly time spent on the phone and 171% in money raised. Callers in two control groups, who did not meet the scholarship student, showed no significant changes in performance. In a second study of callers contacting alumni who donated more frequently to the university, the performance effects following a visit from a scholarship recipient were even more striking: A month later, the callers had on average more than doubled their calls per hour and had achieved average weekly revenue increases of more than 400%, from $411.74 to $2,083.52. In a third study, one group of callers met with a scholarship recipient, another met with a manager who described a student who had benefited from the callers' efforts, and a third group had no intervention. Only the first group experienced any performance improvement.

The Art of Motivation Maintenance

The high-burnout field of fundraising might feel like an extreme example, but my research suggests that outsourcing inspiration is effective in a wide range of settings. Three basic mechanisms are at work. The first is *impact:* Employees see for themselves how their work benefits others. This is readily apparent in companies whose products save lives. At Medtronic's annual holiday party, for instance, patients are invited to share their stories about how the company's medical technologies helped them. The stories humanize the work for the engineers and technicians behind the scenes. But employees who make less dramatic contributions can also be inspired by real-life examples of the impact of their work. At Wells Fargo, when bankers hear a customer describe how a loan has enabled her to buy a house or pay off major debts, they gain a richer understanding of how their work makes a lasting difference.

The second mechanism is *appreciation:* Employees come to feel valued by end users. At Let's Go Publications, where teams of editors revise travel books, managers circulate letters from readers who have relied on the company's advice to navigate foreign countries and experience new cultures. These signs of gratitude let editors know their efforts are appreciated. Similarly, at Olive Garden, leaders share with staff members letters from customers describing how they chose to celebrate meaningful events at the company's restaurants. Even though employees know intellectually that their contributions make a difference, gratitude from end users is a powerful reminder of the value of continued quality improvements and innovation.

The third mechanism is *empathy:* Employees develop a deeper understanding of end users' problems and needs and thereby become more committed to helping them. For example, researchers Rajesh Sethi and Carolyn Nicholson recently found that when product development teams had contact with customers, they were more likely to create offerings that exceeded projections for sales and market share. And at Microsoft, leaders learned that a personal connection can help software developers adopt the perspectives of end users. A Microsoft lab manager interviewed by researchers Michael Cusumano and Richard Selby explains that after seeing an end user, developers "immediately empathize with the person. The usual nonsense answer—'Well, they can just look in the manual if they don't know how to use it,' or 'My idea is brilliant; you just found ten stupid people'—that kind of stuff just goes out the door." A face-to-face connection with end users appears to elicit empathy among the developers, motivating them to design software with users in mind.

Even simple reminders of the existence of end users can increase employee motivation. Consider an experiment that David Hofmann and I recently conducted in a hospital. Medical professionals are aware of the importance of hygiene, yet many studies suggest that they wash their hands only about a third as often as they should. We placed signs on units around the hospital near soap and gel dispensers available to doctor and nurses. The first sign read, "Hand hygiene prevents you from catching diseases." The second sign replaced "you" with "patients."

We then tracked soap and gel usage for two weeks after the signs were introduced. We were surprised to find that the second sign yielded average increases of 33% in soap and gel usage, whereas the first sign had no effect. Why? Research shows that medical professionals are overconfident about their immunity to disease but are much more realistic when evaluating the risk to patients, who are often highly vulnerable. This study suggests that a mere mention of end users can make the consequences of one's work more vivid and produce an increase in beneficial behaviors.

A Leader's Guide to Outsourcing Inspiration

Relatively few companies seize opportunities to create motivating connections between employees and end users. Many leaders are simply unaware of those opportunities; others may be concerned about abdicating their roles as visionaries. But as I noted earlier, strong leaders are essential in effectively outsourcing inspiration.

In my recent studies of sales and government employees, I found that inspirational leadership and connections to end users operated in tandem to motivate higher performance, measured in terms of revenue as well as supervisors' ratings. End users complemented rather than substituted for leadership, bringing the leader's vision to life and strengthening employees' beliefs that their contributions mattered.

To outsource inspiration effectively, leaders must build and leverage their networks to find end users, collect their stories, invite them to the organization, introduce them to employees, and recognize workers' contributions. How can they accomplish this?

Identify past, present, and future end users

Many leaders mistakenly assume that they know who their end users are. For example, researcher Michael Tushman writes of senior managers at a large food products company that sold jars of pureed, strained, and chopped foods, such as meats, fruits, and vegetables. The managers were marketing the jars as baby food, assuming that their customers were parents of infants. But during a routine trip to a grocery store, one of the Florida sales team members discovered a hidden end user: elderly people, who were buying the products because they needed food that was easy to eat and digest. In addition to opening up a new market segment, this discovery alerted the company to a new category of end user who valued the company's products. To connect with the broadest possible range of end users, ask leaders, managers, and employees at different levels of the organization to identify various groups of clients, customers, suppliers, patients, and other recipients who have benefited, currently benefit, or could benefit from the work that employees do.

Dig up feedback from past end users

Many organizations regularly collect useful information from focus groups and customer surveys that ends up trapped in silos or viewed strictly as marketing research to facilitate customer outreach and product development. This kind of feedback, no matter how old, can provide powerful examples of a company's impact on

49

When You Can't Find End Users

CONNECTIONS BETWEEN EMPLOYEES AND END USERS are most powerful when they are face-to-face. How can leaders build those connections when they lack access to end users or can't find any with inspiring stories? Research suggests three options:

1. **Show pictures.** Even a snapshot of an end user can be powerfully motivating. Consider the case of radiologists who study x-rays to diagnose illness without ever meeting the patients. A study by Yehonatan Turner and colleagues showed that radiologists who saw photos of patients increased the length of their reports by 29% and improved the accuracy of their diagnoses by 46%. Microfinance organization Kiva uses the same approach, showing potential donors pictures of the social entrepreneurs requesting funding.

   A note about choosing effective photos: Research by Deborah Small and Nicole Verrochi suggests that people are more likely to empathize with end users who appear sad or neutral and thus may be signaling an unfulfilled need.

2. **Circulate inside stories.** When employees share with one another their stories about experiences with end users, they can create a venue for mutual inspiration. At Ritz-Carlton hotels around the world, employees meet daily for 15 minutes to share "wow" stories about going the

end users. For example, when Bob Austin joined Volvo in 1970 as a customer service representative, he received many unsolicited letters from people who had been in accidents and were writing to say that medical professionals and police officers had told them that they would have been killed if they had not been driving a Volvo. Two decades later, Austin became the head of public relations and created a club for Volvo drivers who believed that one of the automaker's cars had saved their lives. He tracked down past letters and invited the customers to join the club. Since then, Volvo's contributions to customers' lives have been more visible. Similarly, in my studies with fundraising callers, I discovered that the organization had a database of thank-you letters from grateful scholarship recipients. Managers had simply never considered sharing the letters with the callers.

extra mile to make a difference in customers' lives. In sharing these tales, employees inspire not only one another but also themselves. It turns out that the simple act of sharing a story about benefiting others can reinforce one's conviction about the purpose of a job. In one study, Jane Dutton and I found that employees who kept a weekly journal about how their work made a difference worked harder and achieved higher performance.

3. **Share outside stories.** Employees such as bank examiners, airline pilots, and nuclear power plant workers do jobs that are designed to protect people, but they rarely see the impact of their work. Stories from outsiders can help. When I gave lifeguards a few short news stories about other lifeguards who had rescued swimmers, they showed improvements in the month following: They viewed their jobs as more meaningful and valued, volunteered to work more hours, and spent more time and energy protecting the safety of swimmers—as measured by their supervisor's ratings. Lifeguards who read stories about only the personal benefits of the job showed no improvements. The director was stunned. Lifeguards surely know that their actions can save lives, but they don't feel it viscerally and emotionally until they're directly exposed to vivid examples of how their work can affect living, breathing human beings.

Seek out new stories

When employees lack a strong sense of impact, appreciation, and empathy, or when a particular group of end users is invisible, managers and employees can go into the field. At Medtronic, more than two-thirds of procedures using the company's medical devices are attended by an engineer, salesperson, or technician. As former Medtronic CEO Bill George explained to me: "Employees need to remember when they get frustrated that they're here to restore people to full life and health. If I'm making semiconductors, how do I get to see the impact on patients? If I'm doing software development and there's a glitch in a defibrillator, people could be harmed or killed. Put it in those terms, work becomes very personal . . . It's very important that employees get out there and see procedures . . . it's a way of communicating what we're all about."

Of course, these stories are most effective when they are shared not as vehicles for maximizing the bottom line but as genuine efforts to bring greater meaning to the work. Leaders who consider it their moral responsibility to help employees see the actual and potential consequences of their work are likely to inspire their employees; those who attempt to connect with end users just for a performance boost risk fostering cynicism and skepticism among the workforce.

Set up events and meetings where end users can share their experiences

My research shows that although stories and letters can be motivating, a face-to-face connection with end users has a stronger emotional impact on employees. These sessions are most inspiring when they include end users whom employees do not normally see. For example, Deere & Company invites farmers who are buying tractors to visit the factories with their families. Assembly line employees get to meet the farmers, hand them a gold key, and watch them start their tractors for the first time. At Raytheon, military troops speak at divisional meetings, describing how a division's product saved their lives. An employee reflected that "putting names, faces, and stories with the individuals using our products certainly portrayed the point of our mission." (See the sidebar "When You Can't Find End Users" to learn how to outsource inspiration when face-to-face meetings aren't possible.)

Turn employees into end users

Employees who have little experience with the company's products or services often contribute more after they spend some time in customers' shoes. For example, at Four Seasons Hotels, employee orientations conclude with a "familiarization stay" in which housekeepers and clerks spend a night in their own hotels to experience the service firsthand. As a vice president of learning and development explained, "They're learning what it looks like to receive service from the other side." At outdoor gear company Cabela's, retail employees can borrow fishing and camping equipment and write a review, which helps them understand the customer's perspective.

Find end users inside the organization

Internal end users—such as a customer-facing team audited by backroom accountants or investment bankers who give client presentations prepared by junior consultants and analysts—are prime sources of feedback. For example, Francesca Gino and I found that when a manager from another department visited a call center to thank employees for their contributions, those employees increased their effort by 51% during the following week, whereas employees in a control group did not. Connecting with internal customers can be a powerful step toward reducing misconceptions and conflict between groups and departments.

Engage employees who currently do low-impact work

Finding ways to connect end users to employees who seem to deliver few direct, lasting benefits can require a bit more creativity. One way is to leverage their unique knowledge and expertise. For example, Best Buy has created Twelpforce, a service that lets employees across the company, regardless of their job descriptions, use X/Twitter to respond to customers' questions and inquiries. In its first year, more than 2,600 Best Buy employees from across the company—including those who did not normally play customer-facing roles—joined Twelpforce and responded to more than 27,000 inquiries. At Whole Foods, employees whose jobs involve unpacking boxes and stocking shelves have the opportunity to educate shoppers about allergies, organic food quality standards, sustainable agriculture, and environmental preservation and recycling; some even teach cooking classes. Of course, it is important to make sure that employees have the knowledge, skills, and time to take on new responsibilities.

Spread the message

Outsourcing inspiration is in large part a communications task. It is useful to organize events with end users, create videos, and post their stories on websites and intranets. For example, St. Luke's Hospital hosts a Night of Heroes event, during which patients are reconnected with the trauma teams that saved their lives and all team

Homer Simpson or Ned Flanders: Which Employees Are Most Motivated by End Users?

ARE ALL EMPLOYEES EQUALLY MOTIVATED by seeing their impact on end users? Not necessarily.

Consider the personality trait of conscientiousness: the degree to which people are responsible, disciplined, and goal-oriented (think Ned Flanders from *The Simpsons* animated TV series) versus carefree and spontaneous (think Homer Simpson). One might assume that highly conscientious employees, because they prize dependability and responsibility, would care more about connecting with end users. In a recent study, however, I found the exact opposite to be the case. The Ned Flanders types tend to operate at a high motivational ceiling, performing well regardless of feedback. The Homer Simpsons, on the other hand, depend heavily on external cues about why their work is important.

The good news is that connections with end users are most effective with the very employees who most need to be motivated.

members are honored for their contributions. Senior leaders speak at the event, demonstrating its importance.

Recognize high-impact contributions
Because leaders are often unaware of episodes of excellent customer service, coworkers can help identify them. Zappos, Google, Southwest Airlines, and Linden Lab all have peer bonus and recognition programs in which employees can commend and reward coworkers who have made outstanding contributions. When stories about these contributions go viral, they can be particularly potent: Spontaneity can signal that colleagues are genuinely motivated to make a difference.

Outsourcing inspiration can have a significant, lasting effect on employees' motivation, performance, and productivity. When customers, clients, and patients describe how a company's products and services make a difference, they bring a leader's vision to life in a credible, memorable way. Employees can vividly understand the impact of their work, see how their contributions are appreciated by end users, and experience stronger concern for them. By connecting employees to end users, leaders can motivate through their actions, not only their words. Their inspirational messages become more than lip service.

Originally published in June 2011. Reprint R1106G

The Dual-Purpose Playbook

by Julie Battilana, Anne-Claire Pache, Metin Sengul, and Marissa Kimsey

CORPORATIONS ARE BEING PUSHED to change—to dial down their single-minded pursuit of financial gain and pay closer attention to their impact on employees, customers, communities, and the environment. Corporate social responsibility from the sidelines is no longer enough, and the pressure comes from various directions: rising and untenable levels of inequality, increasing evidence that the effects of climate change will be devastating, investors' realization that short-term profitability and long-term sustainability are sometimes in conflict. For reasons like these, a growing number of business leaders now understand that they must embrace both financial and social goals.

However, changing an organization's DNA is extraordinarily difficult. How can a company that has always focused on profit balance the two aims? It takes upending the existing business model. Not surprisingly, researchers have consistently found that companies are quick to abandon social goals in the quest for profitability.

Yet some enterprises successfully pursue both. The U.S. outdoor-clothing company Patagonia, for example, which initially prioritized financial goals, has come to pursue social good more seriously over time. Others began with social goals but must earn revenue to survive. Grameen Bank, the Nobel Prize–winning microlender in Bangladesh, is an iconic example. We've spent a decade studying how socially driven businesses succeed, and what we've learned from in-depth qualitative studies and quantitative analyses may prove useful to traditional companies that want to adopt a dual purpose.

Our research reveals that successful dual-purpose companies have this in common: They take an approach we call *hybrid organizing,* which involves four levers: setting and monitoring social goals alongside financial ones; structuring the organization to support both socially and financially oriented activities; hiring and socializing employees to embrace both; and practicing dual-minded leadership. Taken together, these levers can help companies cultivate and maintain a hybrid culture while giving leaders the tools to productively manage conflicts between social and financial goals when they emerge, making the endeavor more likely to succeed.

Setting Goals, Monitoring Progress

Dual-purpose companies need to set goals along both financial and social dimensions and monitor performance on an ongoing basis.

Setting goals

Well-constructed goals are an essential management tool. They communicate what matters and can highlight what's working and what's not. These goals should go beyond mere aspirations to clarify a company's dual purpose for employees, customers, suppliers, investors, and regulators. Companies may need to experiment their way to a goal-setting model that works for them—something Grameen Veolia Water has managed by continually recalibrating its activities around explicit aims.

The company, which provides safe water in Bangladesh, started in 2008 as a joint venture between Grameen Bank and the water services provider Veolia. Veolia, which traditionally works under government contracts, recognized that no local authorities were responsible for providing drinking water to rural areas at that time.

Idea in Brief

The Problem

Corporations are being pushed to dial down their single-minded pursuit of financial gain and pay closer attention to their impact on society. But how can a company balance the two?

The Research

The authors have studied companies around the globe that pursue financial and social goals simultaneously. They find that the successful ones build a commit-

ment to both economic and social value into their core organizational activities.

The Solution

Companies that want to do well and do good should focus on four key management practices: setting and monitoring dual goals; structuring the organization to support both goals; hiring and socializing employees to embrace them; and practicing dual-minded leadership.

The partnership aimed to fill this gap. Its board set two goals for the new business at the outset: to provide safe, affordable drinking water to the inhabitants of the rural villages of Goalmari and Padua over the long term, and to sustain operations from sales without relying on grants.

These two goals came into conflict. When managers realized how difficult it would be to break even if they sold water only to poor rural households at a very low price, they designed a new revenue-generating activity: selling water in jars to schools and businesses in nearby urban areas. At this point it might have been tempting to focus attention and resources on the profitable new market segment at the expense of the original one. But leadership did not drift. The venture's clearly stated social goal reminded board members and managers that urban sales were meant to subsidize village sales. Ultimately the former amounted to half the company's revenues, helping Grameen Veolia Water pursue its social goal.

No single playbook exists for setting social goals. But our studies point to two rules of thumb. First, *do the research.* Often leaders try to set goals without developing a deep understanding of the specific social needs they aim to address—or of how they may have contributed in the past to the buildup of problems. Just as they conduct market research to identify opportunities for profit, they should study those social needs. Their research should involve the intended beneficiaries along with other stakeholders and experts.

Prior to launching operations, Grameen Veolia Water conducted major research to understand water issues in Bangladesh, interviewing public officials and health and water experts along with community organizations. Managers discovered that some rural populations suffered not only from drinking surface water contaminated with bacteria (the researchers' initial assumption) but also from drinking water from wells built in the 1980s. Some well water, although clear and tasteless, was naturally contaminated by arsenic and was a major source of cancers in adults and cognitive impairment in children. This information led the business to focus its activity in Goalmari and Padua, which suffered from both sources of contamination. The company thus defined its goal as providing permanent access to clean water for everyone in those villages.

Second, *set goals that are explicit and enduring* (though they may have to be updated in light of a changing environment). Impact would be limited if the village residents consumed clean water for just a few years; to achieve a significant positive change in their health, they would need access to clean water over decades.

Monitoring progress

Just as important as setting goals is identifying and adapting key performance indicators (KPIs) in order to measure the achievement of specific targets, be they financial or social. While we know how to measure sales, revenue growth, and return on assets, no widely accepted metrics currently exist for many social goals (although more progress has been made on measuring environmental impact). Nonetheless, it is possible to set both financial and social KPIs successfully. Our research has found that companies succeed by dedicating substantial time and effort to developing a manageable number of trackable metrics during the goal-setting process and revisiting them regularly to assess their continuing relevance and adequacy.

At Grameen Veolia Water, managers consulted with members of the rural communities they sought to serve and with academic experts before formalizing four KPIs: the company's self-financing ratio (its ability to fund planned investments from its own resources), the number of villagers with access to its services, the rate of rural penetration, and the rate of rural regular consumption (which captures both financial and social performance). The four numbers are updated monthly to monitor operations, and the board discusses them quarterly to guide strategic decision-making.

A learning mindset is essential for developing and using KPIs. A willingness to experiment and change on the basis of experience, whether their own or others', helps businesses better understand social problems and how to address them. Dimagi's approach to setting social performance metrics exemplifies this mindset. Founded in 2002 and led by Jonathan Jackson, one of its cofounders, Dimagi provides software that NGOs and governments can use to develop mobile apps for frontline health-care workers in developing countries. At first Dimagi's primary social metric was the number of active users, which was meant to indicate how many people the technology positively affected. Jackson hoped to improve this metric, because it failed to distinguish between those who actually used the data to improve service delivery to patients and those who collected but did nothing with it.

The company formed a dedicated impact team to refine the social KPI. After exploration, the team created a metric—"worker activity months"—to measure the number of health-care providers who were actually applying Dimagi's technology, and it implemented internal data systems to track the metric across all projects. But Jackson soon realized that this, too, was flawed, because the outcome was beyond Dimagi's control: How workers used the software depended more on the actions of Dimagi's clients—NGOs and governments—than on its own.

After reaching out to other social enterprises for advice, Jackson reverted to the number of active users as the company's primary social barometer, yet combined it with a new entity—an impact review team—that focused on qualitative quarterly analyses and discussions about the impact of all projects. These reviews ensure that a team doesn't focus unduly on the quantifiable aspects of a project (revenue, costs, completion dates) but also explores the effectiveness of its service delivery and how that could be improved to better support frontline health-care workers. The team discusses indirect forms of impact as well, such as helping organizations assess their readiness for digitization.

Other successful businesses also complement KPIs with in-depth qualitative assessments of their social performance. For example, the Brazilian impact investing firm Vox Capital hired Jéssica Silva Rios, an executive dedicated to understanding and measuring its impact, and recently made her a full partner. Some companies also incorporate external social indicators developed by independent NGOs such as the Global Reporting Initiative, the Sustainability Accounting Standards Board, and B Lab. For example, Vox Capital monitors whether its rating from the Global Impact Investing Rating System is above average in comparison with other funds in developing markets and adjusts the fees it charges investors accordingly.

Structuring the Organization

It's virtually impossible to succeed on financial and social fronts over the long run if the company isn't designed to support both. Achieving an effective design requires that you think about which organizational activities create economic value and which create social value, how those activities relate to one another, and how you'll try to balance them.

Aligning activities and structure

Some activities create social and economic value at the same time. Others create predominantly one kind of value. For activities that create both kinds, an integrated organizational structure usually makes sense. Otherwise the activities are often best managed separately.

Revolution Foods, founded in 2006 by Kristin Richmond and Kirsten Tobey, provides nutritious lunches to low-income students in the United States. Richmond and Tobey created the company to serve a social purpose, having witnessed how poor food options hold kids back in underfunded schools. Every time they sell a healthful meal to a school, two things happen: They enhance a child's health, and they make money. Their core activity thus creates both kinds of value. As a result, they opted for an integrated structure, with a single manager in charge of operational efficiency, business growth, and the promotion of child well-being. Account managers often engage students in nutrition education (either directly or through community organizations), introducing them to new foods and collecting their feedback on taste. The exposure to healthful foods enhances the long-term wellness of students and supports sales at the same time.

In contrast, the French company ENVIE learned over time that it needed to decouple the two kinds of activities. Launched in 1984, it had the goal of reintegrating long-term unemployed people into the job market by hiring them on two-year contracts to collect and repair used appliances for sale in secondhand shops. The company also provides support and training in how to repair appliances, how to look for a job, how to write a CV, and how to interview. The resale of appliances is what creates economic value. The training to enhance individuals' ability to find jobs outside ENVIE creates social value, but it doesn't make the company more profitable—in fact, it increases costs.

In the early years, staff members were asked to do two jobs: give beneficiaries technical guidance on how to repair or dismantle appliances (economic value) and provide them with social support (social value). However, it was difficult to find supervisors with both social and technical expertise. Even when they had both, the supervisors struggled to balance the two dimensions of their jobs. ENVIE's founders accordingly decided to set up separate organizational units, one for social support and one for repair, to be overseen by social workers and technical experts respectively. This increased the company's effectiveness in generating both kinds of value.

Creating spaces of negotiation

The rub is that tensions inevitably arise—particularly in differentiated structures. Left unattended, they can bring an organization to a halt. The Bolivian microlender Banco Solidario provides a cautionary example. In the 1990s constant resentment and fighting between bankers (concerned with fees and efficiency) and social workers (concerned with the affordability of loans and the livelihoods of microentrepreneurs) essentially froze the company. Loan officers quit left and right, the number of active borrowers plummeted, and the profit margin dropped. We've found that successful dual-purpose companies avoid such paralysis by supplementing traditional organizational structures with mechanisms for surfacing and working through tensions. These mechanisms don't make the tensions disappear—rather, they bring them into the open by letting employees actively discuss trade-offs between creating economic value and creating social value. Such deliberation provides a powerful safety valve and can speed up effective resolution.

Consider Vivractif, another French work-integration company. Founded in 1993, it hires and trains the long-term unemployed at recycling facilities. Those responsible for achieving one kind of goal or the other at the company often did not see eye to eye. While production supervisors managed workers to meet recycling targets, social workers were eager to take them away from the floor for mentorship and job-search training. The company set up quarterly meetings between the two groups so that they could discuss each beneficiary's progress and bring up coordination issues. Joint work planning allowed both to share important deadlines (such as for commercial deliveries or social trainings) and to find joint solutions to scheduling conflicts. This improved productivity and furthered the company's social goals.

Spaces of negotiation can be successful in large companies as well. In one multinational cooperative bank headquartered in Europe, decision-makers representing each of the local branches collectively make strategic decisions only after iterative debate, during which different groups of employees are responsible for championing either the social or the financial objectives of the organization. When individuals speak up about issues, their assigned roles prevent tensions from becoming personal.

Hiring and Socializing Employees

Embedding a dual-purpose focus in an organization's DNA requires a workforce with shared values, behaviors, and processes. Hiring and socialization are crucial to getting that right.

Hiring

Employees in a company that pursues dual goals tend to be successful when they understand and connect with both the business and the social mission. We've seen companies mobilize such people by recruiting three types of profiles: hybrid, specialized, and "blank slate."

Hybrid individuals arrive equipped with training or experience in both business and social-value fields, such as environmental science, medicine, social work, and so forth. Such people are able to understand issues in both camps and can connect with employees and other stakeholders of either orientation.

Jean-François Connan is a good example. He was recruited in the late 1980s by Adecco, one of the largest temp work groups in the world, because he had training in industrial maintenance and human resources and experience as a teacher and a mentor for at-risk youth. The company hired him to help address a long-standing problem: A large number of its temp workers lacked strong qualifications. Connan played a leading role in building a dual-purpose subsidiary for Adecco that helps the long-term unemployed reenter the job market by hiring them for temp jobs. His background lets him interact seamlessly with Adecco leaders and corporate clients as well as with local partners (such as nonprofits dedicated to youth mentorship) and those whom they seek to serve. Now he is the company's head of responsibility and social innovation.

But hybrid employees aren't always available and may not always be the best fit. Dual-purpose corporations often hire *specialized* talent, which allows them to tap into deep expertise and networks in each area. The main weakness of this approach is that it is more likely to result in conflict between groups, which may not understand each other's norms, vocabularies, and constraints—especially if the organization separates economic activities from social ones. As a result, tensions and turnover in these companies tend to be higher than in those with an integrated structure, producing a negative effect on the bottom line.

To mitigate this at Dimagi, Jackson explains the primacy of the organization's social purpose on his very first recruitment call with a technical expert (such as a software developer). After hiring, he creates opportunities for the expert to learn about the social business through formal talks, informal office interactions, and even face-to-face fieldwork in the underserved communities with which Dimagi works. Vox Capital, too, has hired managers with technical capabilities (such as fund management) and no experience in a social-mission-driven environment. Yet it systematically screens applicants for their ability to embrace and thus adapt to the company's hybrid culture.

When companies recruit *blank slate* individuals, who have experience in neither business nor the social sector, they put them in entry-level jobs and help them acquire dual values and skills. The Bolivian microcredit lender Los Andes S.A. Caja de Ahorro y Préstamo, founded in 1995, took this approach, hiring university graduates with hardly any professional experience to become loan officers. The sense was that they would embrace a hybrid organizational culture more readily than experienced employees might. Of course, this approach has limitations. Taking inexperienced staffers into an organization may lower productivity. It also requires a considerable investment in training.

Although recruitment strategies obviously must be adapted to specific HR needs, we have observed that hybrid employees tend to be particularly well-suited for managerial and coordination positions; specialists can contribute useful expertise as middle managers in differentiated structures; and blank slates do best in entry-level jobs, where training won't be too challenging.

Socialization
Once people are on board, socializing them can be daunting. Every employee needs to understand, value, and become capable of contributing to both financial and social goals in some form.

Formal approaches to socialization may include companywide events such as annual general assemblies and retreats where dual goals and values are explained, discussed, assessed, and put into perspective. Dedicated trainings can remind employees—particularly those who specialize in just one sector—of the interconnectedness of revenue-generating and social-value-creating activities. Job-shadowing programs and other forms of experiential training can also purposefully bring different groups together. At Vivractif social workers spend at least one day a year alongside recycling supervisors, and vice versa, so that each can learn and relearn about the company from the other perspective.

Another example comes from Oftalmología salauno, a Mexican company cofounded in 2011 by Javier Okhuysen and Carlos Orellana to provide high-quality, low-cost eye care to people who can't otherwise afford it. Although the pair saw economic goals and social goals as connected, they observed that some doctors focused only on patient care, and some managers considered only costs. So they formulated a set of core tenets and shared them at a daylong training for all employees, which clarified the interrelatedness of the company's financial and social aspects and gave employees a shared language for discussing tensions. Okhuysen and Orellana later instituted such sessions for new hires and continue to reinforce the training content in day-to-day interactions.

Spaces of negotiation can be valuable informal socialization opportunities, too. At Vox Capital a weekly time slot allows anyone to pose a question if he or she feels that the company's practices don't align with the organizational mission and values or is witnessing financial-social trade-offs. Employees haven't shied away from tough topics. Some have asked whether its investment portfolio sufficiently emphasizes the social missions of the businesses, while others have questioned whether the company's approach to raising capital is ethical.

Such conversations pushed cofounder Daniel Izzo to think critically about Vox's principles. "First I thought, It doesn't matter as long as [investors] don't have a say in what we do," he says. "But then someone asked, 'Would you take a drug lord as an investor?' Of course not. So there is a line. But where do we draw it? Do you take money from companies involved in corruption scandals in Brazil? Or from sons and daughters of top executives in those companies?"

Similarly, Bernardo Bonjean, who founded the Brazilian microfinance organization Avante in 2012, instituted a monthly breakfast where employees could come together and ask him questions. He also shares what's on his mind in letters to employees, discussing everything from the company's KPIs to his concerns about cash flow in the coming months. Okhuysen and Orellana put posters showing a matrix of Oftalmología salauno's four core tenets—commitment, service, reach, and value—in every meeting room. They can refer to these tenets when decision points arise, supporting a shared language among employees.

To encourage questions from employees, it's important to create an environment where people feel safe raising contentious issues. And when employees see changes in thinking and processes result from these discussions, they know that what they say is valued.

Events and conversations aren't the only ways to socialize employees. Promotion and compensation are also important. At the multinational cooperative bank mentioned above, being promoted to general director of a local branch requires excelling in business development, cost reduction, and profit making while also demonstrating a clear adherence to the company's social goals and a willingness to work collaboratively. One candidate for promotion commented, "I have seen many brilliant people fail because they did not embrace our values enough."

Vox Capital, like several other companies we studied, bases individual bonuses on both financial and social performance. Furthermore, Izzo is clear that he does not want the economic inequality that Vox is trying to redress in Brazil reproduced inside the company itself, so the maximum difference between employees' highest and lowest salaries and bonuses is capped at a multiple of 10. (In the United States in 2017 the average ratio of CEO-to-worker compensation was 312:1, according to the Economic Policy Institute.) Other companies, such as Revolution Foods, use shared ownership to motivate employees and increase their commitment to dual performance. Any full-time employee can become a shareholder through stock options. Richmond and Tobey believe that sharing ownership with employees, many of whom live in the low-income communities the company serves, is integral to their social mission.

Practicing Dual-Minded Leadership

Leaders must manage the tensions that inevitably crop up on the path to achieving dual goals. These tensions often involve competition for resources and divergent views about how to reach those goals. Leaders must affirm, embody, and protect both the financial and the social side and address tensions proactively.

Making decisions

Strategic decisions should embody dual goals. Whereas goals reflect aspirations, decisions provide real evidence of leaders' commitment to achieving specific aims. The experience of François-Ghislain Morillon and Sébastien Kopp is a good example.

Morillon and Kopp created Veja in 2004 to sell sneakers made under fair trade and environmentally friendly conditions in small cooperatives in Brazil. When they realized that advertising accounted for 70% of the cost of a typical major brand's sneakers, they made the bold decision not to advertise at all. That allowed them to sell sneakers at a price comparable to what their bigger competitors asked despite having production costs five to seven times as high. To make up for the absence of traditional advertising, the company formed strategic partnerships with high-end fashion brands such as agnès b. and Madewell and stores such as the Galeries Lafayette to increase media exposure, grow sales, and become profitable.

At first Veja's clients—shoe retailers accustomed to the marketing of major sneaker brands—were skeptical. So Veja trained salespeople to educate them about the benefits of its product for people and the environment. Clients and the media now view the "zero ads" decision as evidence of the founders' commitment to their social goals, ultimately both giving the company social impact and making it profitable.

Morillon and Kopp also decided to temper the company's growth, despite increasing consumer demand in the United States. They refused to lower their fair trade and environmental standards to sell more shoes. Instead they decided to set production targets in keeping with the capacity of their fair trade partners while working closely with them to increase that capacity, ensuring a growth rate compatible with financial sustainability. That decision demonstrated, to employees in particular, the genuine commitment of Veja's leaders to their dual goals. In making bold decisions, the cofounders both emphasized the company's priorities and created the conditions for achieving them. They also showed that it's possible to avoid one of the most common pitfalls for dual-purpose companies: prioritizing profits over society when the pressure is on.

Profit allocation is another important area of strategic decision-making. Dividends can be capped to ensure that financial goals don't overshadow social ones. When founding Oftalmología salauno, Okhuysen and Orellana pledged to reinvest 100% of their profits for at least seven years, so the investors they selected—a social impact fund, the World Bank, and a private wealth-management fund— knew that no dividends would be paid during that time. Okhuysen explains: "Our investors ultimately expect both financial and social returns on their capital. But the alignment between us around reinvesting profits to improve and grow our network of eye-care clinics has helped ensure that financial goals do not take precedence over our social purpose."

Engaging the board

In successful hybrid companies, board members serve as guardians of the dual purpose. Thus they must collectively bring a combination of business and social expertise to the table. Diversity on the board is important for drawing the organization's attention to both social and financial goals, yet it increases the risk of conflict, because members with different perspectives are more likely to differ as to the best course of action. We have seen some companies experience near-paralyzing governance crises when socially and commercially minded board members with similar levels of influence strongly disagree.

Yet other companies have managed to avoid such crises because a chair or an executive director systematically bridged gaps between the two groups. By fostering regular interactions and information sharing between them, such leaders enabled the groups to develop mutual understanding. Recall the subsidiary Jean-François Connan founded at Adecco. He invited representatives from prominent local nonprofits to join the board as minority shareholders, enabling the company to benefit from their social expertise, networks, and legitimacy and helping to protect the company's social mission. His hybrid experience put Connan in a good position to bridge the gap between the two groups of directors, fostering common ground by constantly reminding each of the importance of the other.

Some major roadblocks to dual-purpose organizing are outside a company's control. Chief among them is that the business ecosystem is still set up to prioritize the creation of shareholder wealth. The Global Reporting Initiative, the Sustainability Accounting Standards Board, and B Lab, among others, have taken steps to overcome some of these barriers. Each of them has created metrics for tracking companies' impact on the lives of employees and customers, the communities served, and the environment, providing organizations with benchmarks. What is at stake is ensuring that companies don't pick and choose areas of social focus on the basis of convenience.

Rating agencies are only one part of the ecosystem, however. Although more changes are under way—such as awarding legal status to public benefit corporations in the United States, community interest companies in the United Kingdom, and *società benefit* in Italy—the regulations, educational standards, investment models, and norms that govern the production of economic value and social value are still mostly distinct from one another. As an increasing number of companies engage in hybrid organizing, the systems that support business also need to change.

But changing organizations and the ecosystem that surrounds them is difficult. Companies must fight the inertia of inherited ways of thinking and behaving. Trade-offs and tensions are inevitable, and success is more likely when leaders address them head-on. The four levers we have outlined are meant to help.

Originally published in March–April 2019. Reprint R1902K

The New CEO Activists

by Aaron K. Chatterji and Michael W. Toffel

WHEN WE FIRST STARTED STUDYING CEO ACTIVISM, three years ago, we never imagined how significant this phenomenon would become. At the time a small but growing band of executives were taking public stands on political and social issues unrelated to their companies' bottom lines. Since then, controversies over laws affecting transgender people in North Carolina, police shootings in Missouri, and executive orders on immigration have drawn increasing numbers of CEOs into contentious public debates. More recently, the White House's withdrawal from the Paris climate accord, response to the clash between white supremacists and counterprotesters in Charlottesville, Virginia, and decision to rescind Deferred Action for Childhood Arrivals have galvanized many U.S. corporate leaders to speak out and take action.

Of course, corporations have long played an active role in the U.S. political process. They lobby, make contributions to candidates, and fund political action committees and campaigns on various issues in an effort to shape public policies to their benefit. But CEO activism is something new. Until recently, it was rare for corporate leaders to plunge aggressively into thorny social and political discussions about race, sexual orientation, gender, immigration, and the environment. The so-called Michael Jordan dictum that Republicans buy sneakers too reminds executives that choosing sides on divisive issues can hurt sales, so why do it? Better to weigh in on what traditionally have been seen as business issues, such as taxes and trade, with technocratic arguments rather than moral appeals.

But the world has changed. Political partisanship and discourse grow ever more extreme, and the gridlock in Washington, D.C., shows no sign of easing. Political and social upheaval has provoked frustration and outrage, inspiring business leaders like Tim Cook of Apple, Howard Schultz of Starbucks, and Marc Benioff of Salesforce—among many others—to passionately advocate for a range of causes. "Our jobs as CEOs now include driving what we think is right," Bank of America's CEO, Brian Moynihan, told the *Wall Street Journal*. "It's not exactly political activism, but it is action on issues beyond business."

The world is taking notice. CEO activism has gotten lots of media attention lately, and public relations firms are now building entire practices around it. While this phenomenon has largely been confined to the United States, there's little reason to doubt that it could develop into a global force. We believe that the more CEOs speak up on social and political issues, the more they will be expected to do so. And increasingly, CEO activism has strategic implications: In the X/Twitter age, silence is more conspicuous—and more consequential.

All this activity raises big questions that we will attempt to address: Does CEO activism actually change hearts and minds? What are the risks and potential rewards? And what is the playbook for corporate leaders considering speaking out?

Why CEOs Speak Up

CEOs are weighing in on controversial topics for several reasons. Some point to their corporate values to explain their advocacy, as BOA's Moynihan and Dan Schulman of PayPal did when taking a stand against a North Carolina law requiring people to use the bathrooms corresponding with the gender on their birth certificates, which became a referendum on transgender rights.

Other CEOs argue that companies should have a higher purpose beyond maximizing shareholder value—a concept that has been

Idea in Brief

The Situation

More and more CEOs are taking a stand on divisive social issues—a dramatic departure from tradition.

The Reason

They're frustrated with the growing political turmoil and paralysis in the government. Stakeholders,

furthermore, are starting to expect corporate leaders to speak out.

The Upshot

CEO activism can have unintended consequences. In this article, the authors look at recent examples of such advocacy and piece together a playbook for executives.

gaining traction in the business world. As Benioff told *Time*, "Today CEOs need to stand up not just for their shareholders, but their employees, their customers, their partners, the community, the environment, schools, everybody."

And for many leaders, speaking out is a matter of personal conviction. David Green, the founder and CEO of Hobby Lobby, a family-owned chain of crafts stores, cited his religious beliefs when opposing the Obamacare requirement that health insurance for employees include coverage for the morning-after pill among all other forms of birth control.

Some leaders have commented that a greater sense of corporate purpose has become important to Millennials, whether they be employees or customers. Indeed, research from Weber Shandwick and KRC Research finds that large percentages of Millennials believe that CEOs have a responsibility to speak out on political and social issues and say that CEO activism is a factor in their purchasing decisions.

Sometimes leaders point to multiple motivations. "I just think it's insincere to not stand up for those things that you believe in," Jeff Immelt, the former CEO of GE, has said. "We're also stewards of our companies; we're representatives of the people that work with us. And I think we're cowards if we don't take a position occasionally on those things that are really consistent with what our mission is and where our people stand."

The Tactics of CEO Activists

Though they're motivated by diverse interests—external, internal, and deeply personal—activist CEOs generally employ two types of tactics: raising awareness and leveraging economic power.

Raising awareness

For the most part, this involves making public statements—often in the news media, more frequently on X/Twitter—to garner support for social movements and help usher in change. In such statements business leaders are communicating to stakeholders where they stand on a whole slate of issues that would not have been on the CEO's agenda a generation ago. For example, Goldman Sachs's CEO, Lloyd Blankfein, and Biogen's former CEO George Scangos have spoken out publicly on government policies that affect the rights of LGBTQ individuals. On the socially conservative side of the spectrum, Chick-fil-A's CEO, Dan Cathy, has denounced gay marriage.

How CEOs respond: Three types of tactics

Traditional	Nonconfrontational
	Lobby behind the scenes
	Contribute to campaigns
	Communicate internally with employees
	Do nothing
Activism	**Raising awareness**
	Issue a statement or tweet
	Write an op-ed
	Seek to spur public action via trade associations
	Exerting economic influence
	Relocate business activities
	Pause business expansion
	Fund political and activist groups

In some cases, several CEOs have worked together to raise awareness. For example, days before the United Nations climate-change-agreement negotiations took place in Paris in late 2015, the CEOs of 14 major food companies—Mars, General Mills, Coca-Cola, Unilever, Danone Dairy North America, Hershey, Ben & Jerry's, Kellogg, PepsiCo, Nestlé USA, New Belgium Brewing, Hain Celestial, Stonyfield Farm, and Clif Bar—cosigned an open letter calling on government leaders to create a strong accord that would "meaningfully address the reality of climate change." Similarly, nearly 100 CEOs cosigned an amicus brief to encourage federal judges to overturn Trump's executive order banning citizens from seven Muslim-majority countries from entering the United States.

Collective action can have greater impact than acting alone. Take what happened with Trump's economic councils. Though Merck's CEO, Kenneth Frazier, received a lot of press when he resigned from the president's American Manufacturing Council in response to Trump's remarks blaming white supremacists and counterprotesters equally for the violence in Charlottesville, it was only after CEOs jumped ship en masse from that group and from Trump's Strategic and Policy Forum that the president disbanded both councils—a move that was widely viewed as a defeat for Trump.

Leveraging economic power

Some of the more powerful cases of CEO activism have involved putting economic pressure on states to reject or overturn legislation. For example, in response to Indiana's Religious Freedom Restoration Act (RFRA), which some viewed as anti-LGBTQ, Bill Oesterle, then the CEO of Angie's List, canceled its planned expansion in Indianapolis, and Benioff threatened to halt all Salesforce employee travel to the state. Other leaders joined the protest, including the president of the National College Athletic Association, Mark Emmert, who suggested that the bill's passage could affect the location of future tournaments and that the association might consider moving its headquarters out of Indianapolis. Under pressure, then-governor Mike Pence approved a revised version of the law, which forbade businesses from denying service to customers because of their sexual orientation.

77

Our Research: Does CEO Activism Influence Public Opinion?

SOME OF THE EXPERIMENTS WE CONDUCTED investigated whether and how CEO activism might affect public opinion. In one, we developed a survey asking people if they supported or opposed Indiana's Religious Freedom Restoration Act (RFRA), at a time when the controversy over it was still very much in the news. In some cases, we first told them that many were concerned that the law might allow discrimination against gays and lesbians. In other cases we attributed those concerns to Apple's CEO, Tim Cook; to Bill Oesterle, who was then CEO of Indiana-based Angie's List; or to the mayor of Indianapolis.

The market research company Civic Science deployed our survey on the hundreds of third-party websites (newspapers, entertainment sites, and so on) with which it partners, gathering 3,418 responses from across the United States. Among those in the baseline condition, who were not told of any discrimination concern, 50% of respondents favored the law—evidence of how split the country is on such legislation. Support for the law dipped to about 40% among respondents who answered the question after being presented with discrimination concerns, regardless of who expressed them—a CEO or a politician—or even if they weren't attributed to anyone in particular.

These results imply that public opinion, at least in this study, was shaped more by the message than by the messenger. There are two ways to interpret this: You can infer that CEOs have no special ability to influence public opinion. After all, their statements had no more effect than politicians' or unattributed statements. On the other hand, the results show that CEOs can be as persuasive as political leaders. CEOs can attract media attention, especially when they speak out on contentious social and environmental issues that are not obviously connected to their bottom lines, which heightens their authenticity. Given that CEOs can sway public opinion, we assume that they can shape public policy, too.

Our study went a bit further to see whether CEO activism would affect people differently depending on their preexisting policy preferences. We found that Cook's discrimination remarks further eroded (already-low) RFRA support among same-sex marriage advocates but had no impact on the much more pro-RFRA views of same-sex marriage opponents. It's important to be aware of whose opinions CEO activism is likely to shift—and whose are likely to be unmoved. In fact, recent research has found that CEOs' political endorsements can significantly affect the campaign contributions of their employees, which suggests that CEO activism might be especially influential with a CEO's own employees.

In response to North Carolina's bathroom law, Schulman canceled PayPal's plans for a new global operations center in Charlotte, which would have created more than 400 skilled jobs. As many other CEOs followed suit, the potential damage mounted: The Associated Press has estimated that the bathroom law controversy will cost the state more than $3.76 billion in lost business over a dozen years.

Companies and their leaders also wield economic power by donating to third-party groups that promote their favored causes. To help fight Trump's immigration ban, for example, the car-sharing company Lyft pledged $1 million to the American Civil Liberties Union, which is challenging the ban in court. In response to the Charlottesville protest and Trump's reaction to it, James Murdoch, the chief executive of 21st Century Fox, donated $1 million to the Anti-Defamation League, a group that fights bigotry.

How effective are these approaches? The trend of corporate leaders taking a public stand on issues not necessarily related to their businesses is relatively new, so there's little empirical evidence of its impact. But we do have limited anecdotal evidence that it can shape public policy—as it did in the case of Indiana's RFRA. When legislators passed a similar religious freedom bill in Georgia, threats to stop filming in the state from leaders of many studios and networks—including Disney, CBS, MGM, and Netflix—and similar kinds of warnings from Benioff and other CEOs were seen as instrumental in moving the governor to veto it. And leaders of the National Basketball Association, NCAA, and Atlantic Coast Conference have been credited with forcing North Carolina to revise its bathroom law.

To move beyond anecdotal evidence, we set out to investigate in a scientific, rigorous way whether CEOs can help win public support for policies, thus affecting legislators' votes and whether governors sign or veto bills. Our findings demonstrate that CEOs can indeed play an important role in shaping the public's views on political and social issues. (See the sidebar "Our Research: Does CEO Activism Influence Public Opinion?") Moreover, as we'll discuss, we find that when CEOs communicate a stance on such issues, it can spur like-minded consumers to purchase more of their products.

The Risks and Potential Rewards

In today's politically charged atmosphere, mere affiliations with political leaders or causes can be risky. A few weeks into Trump's term, Under Armour's CEO, Kevin Plank, faced criticism after referring to the president as "a real asset for the country" in an interview. One of his star pitchmen, the Golden State Warriors player Stephen Curry, expressed his displeasure publicly. The hashtag #BoycottUnderArmour began appearing on X/Twitter, and other Under Armour endorsers, including ballerina Misty Copeland, echoed Curry. The company had to take out a full-page newspaper ad clarifying Plank's comments and stating his opposition to Trump's immigration ban. But that response did not stop Under Armour's stock from being downgraded as one analyst wondered whether the gaffe would "make it nearly impossible to effectively build a cool urban lifestyle brand in the foreseeable future."

CEO activism has sometimes led to charges of hypocrisy. For example, a few conservative websites have criticized Benioff and Cook for denouncing religious freedom laws while Salesforce and Apple continue to do business in countries that persecute LGBTQ individuals. And some activism efforts have come off as clumsy: Consider the widespread ridicule that greeted Howard Schultz's Race Together campaign, in which Starbucks baristas were instructed to write that phrase on all drink cups in an effort to combat racism.

On the other hand, activism can burnish a corporate leader's reputation. In the aftermath of the violence in Charlottesville, the CEOs who resigned from Trump's economic councils (a group that included Plank) were widely praised. The applause for Merck's Frazier, the first to step down, was particularly effusive. "Mr. Frazier, thank you for your courageous stand," tweeted U.S. representative Keith Ellison. The Anne Frank Center for Mutual Respect was even more emphatic, tweeting "A HERO: Ken Frazier."

This controversy also highlighted the risk of silence, which may be viewed as a sign of tacit approval. The *New York Times* and CNBC published lists of which CEOs remained on the president's various economic councils, with CNBC noting that "with each new resignation, those left on the council faced increased scrutiny." Oracle's CEO had similarly been put on the spot when a group of workers from that company launched a petition urging their employer to join numerous other companies in opposing Trump's immigration ban. Their effort attracted national attention, with *USA Today* observing, "More than 130 tech companies—from Apple to Zynga—have signed the amicus brief. Oracle and IBM have not."

Still, CEOs should keep in mind that reactions to activism can cut both ways. While Benioff's advocacy has been widely praised, he admitted to CBS News that Colin Powell, the former secretary of state and a retired four-star general—and now a Salesforce director—warned him: "The farther you go up the tree, the more your backside is going to be exposed, and you'd better be careful." After Chick-fil-A's Cathy spoke out against gay marriage, the chain faced consumer picket lines and a boycott—but also a countervailing "Chick-fil-A Appreciation Day," which attracted large crowds of customers. Indeed, in a Weber Shandwick survey 40% of respondents said they would be more likely to purchase from a company if they agreed with the CEO's position, but 45% said they'd be less likely to if they disagreed with the CEO's view.

We conducted our own experiment to assess the influence of CEO activism on U.S. consumers' behavior. In it, we asked a nationally representative group of respondents about their intent to buy Apple products in the near future. To some, we first provided a statement describing CEO Tim Cook's opinion that Indiana's religious freedom bill was discriminatory against LGBTQ individuals; to others, we provided a generic statement about Cook's management philosophy. To the rest, we provided no statement at all; we simply asked about purchasing intent. We randomly deployed these three conditions and received 2,176 responses. The people in the group exposed to Cook's activism, we found, expressed significantly higher intent to buy Apple products in the near future than those in the other two groups. Learning about Cook's activism increased intent to purchase among supporters of same-sex marriage but did not erode intent among its opponents. These results indicate that CEO activism can generate goodwill for the company but need not alienate those who disagree with the CEO. But this most likely does not apply to all companies. Apple products are especially sticky, so while Cook's remarks might not provoke a backlash against iPhones, other business leaders should consider whether the political makeup of their consumers and the nature of their products might lead to a different result. It's critical for every CEO to proceed thoughtfully.

The CEO Activist's Playbook

Drawing on our empirical research and interviews with CEO activists and their stakeholders, we have developed a guide for leaders who are deciding whether to speak out and how.

What to weigh in on

Smart CEO activists typically choose their issues; the issues do not choose them. To avoid being blindsided by a news story or awkwardly weighing in on a topic they know little about, CEOs should sit down with their executive teams, including their chief communications officers, and decide what issues matter to them and why. This discussion should include reflection on why championing the selected causes would have greater social impact than championing other causes. (On occasion, however, there's no time for this kind of deliberation, such as when corporate leaders felt they quickly needed to make it clear they had no tolerance for racism after Charlottesville.)

Executives must balance the likelihood of having an effect and other potential benefits—such as pleasing employees and consumers—against the possibility of a backlash. As part of this assessment, CEOs should explicitly consider how their statements and actions will be received in a politically polarized atmosphere.

A 2016 Global Strategy Group report shows that when companies are associated with political issues, customers view this connection through the lens of their party affiliation. (See the exhibit "A polarized response.") According to the study, twice as many Democrats viewed Schultz's Race Together campaign positively as

Activism in action

Corporate leader	Issue	Action taken
Marc Benioff CEO, Salesforce	Antidiscrimination	In 2015, Benioff tweeted his opposition to Indiana's Religious Freedom Restoration Act and suspended corporate travel to the state; he later spoke out against North Carolina's bathroom bill and developed a reputation for rallying other business leaders to speak out.
Dan Cathy CEO, Chick-fil-A	Same-sex marriage	In 2012, Cathy publicly opposed same-sex marriage on a radio show; his corporation's foundation also donated to anti-LGBTQ organizations.
David and Barbara Green Cofounders, Hobby Lobby	Health care/religious freedom	The Greens filed a highly publicized lawsuit in 2012 to oppose Affordable Care Act–mandated birth control coverage.
Peter Lewis Late chairman, Progressive Insurance	Marijuana decriminalization	In 2011, Lewis wrote an opinion piece for *Forbes* supporting decriminalization; he also donated $3 million to marijuana legalization campaigns.
John Mackey CEO, Whole Foods Market	Health care	In 2009, Mackey wrote an editorial criticizing the Affordable Care Act.
Paul Polman CEO, Unilever	Climate change	Polman has delivered many public speeches supporting government policies to address climate change.
Jim Rogers Former CEO, Duke Energy	Climate change	In 1990, Rogers (as CEO of Public Service Indiana, which eventually became part of Duke Energy) testified before Congress in support of Clean Air Act amendments; he later lobbied Congress to support climate change legislation.
Hamdi Ulukaya CEO, Chobani	Refugee crisis	In 2014, Ulukaya pledged to donate $2 million to refugees. He also hired refugees to work at Chobani's manufacturing plants and wrote an op-ed for CNN in support of refugees.

Source: Michael W. Toffel, Aaron K. Chatterji, and Julia Kelly, "CEO Activism (A)," Case 617-001 (Boston Harvard Business School, 2017).

viewed it negatively, but three times as many Republicans viewed it unfavorably as viewed it favorably. Cook's advocacy for gay marriage produced similar responses. Championship of less divisive issues, such as parental leave and STEM education, however, is more likely to improve the brand image of the CEO's company among both Democrats and Republicans, the study showed.

CEOs should also consider the extent to which the public believes a CEO voice is appropriate on a given topic. The Global Strategy Group study found that Democrats and Republicans both thought it was fitting for companies to take public stances on economic issues like minimum wage and parental leave. However, there was much less consensus about the appropriateness of weighing in on social issues such as abortion, gun control, LGBTQ equality, and immigration. (See the exhibit "Is it appropriate to take a stand? What consumers think.")

Immigration has proven a particularly complex issue, as the experiences of Chobani's CEO, Hamdi Ulukaya, and Carbonite's CEO, Mohamad Ali, illustrate. Immigrants to the United States themselves, both publicly opposed the Trump administration's restrictions. Both have been praised for their stances, but Ulukaya was also threatened and his company faced a boycott, while Ali's remarks prompted no discernible backlash. This difference could be attributed to Ulukaya's focus on the moral need to provide job opportunities for refugees, whereas Ali placed more emphasis on immigrants as job creators whose work also benefits native-born citizens. It's important to note, however, that while speaking out on controversial topics might provoke an adverse reaction, it is also likely to attract media coverage, which increases the opportunity for a CEO's views to be heard in the first place.

To influence public policy, the message has to be authentic to both the individual leader and the business. There should be a compelling narrative for why *this* issue matters to *this* CEO of *this* business at *this* time. The issue selection is also a crucial time to "get smart" about the underlying details. CEOs can quickly get in over their heads if they start speaking publicly about complex issues and are pressed by knowledgeable journalists and commentators. Because the cred-

A polarized response

Democrats and Republicans can have very different reactions to corporate activism. The chart below shows how each company's stance on a social issue affected its overall favorability ratings with Democrats and Republicans. The percentages indicate the net change in support from members of each party in response to the activist stance.

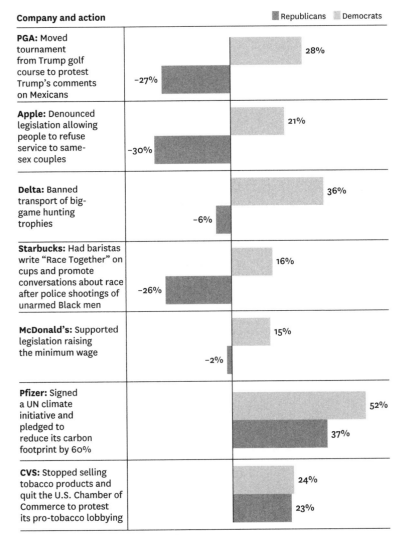

Company and action	Republicans	Democrats
PGA: Moved tournament from Trump golf course to protest Trump's comments on Mexicans	−27%	28%
Apple: Denounced legislation allowing people to refuse service to same-sex couples	−30%	21%
Delta: Banned transport of big-game hunting trophies	−6%	36%
Starbucks: Had baristas write "Race Together" on cups and promote conversations about race after police shootings of unarmed Black men	−26%	16%
McDonald's: Supported legislation raising the minimum wage	−2%	15%
Pfizer: Signed a UN climate initiative and pledged to reduce its carbon footprint by 60%	37%	52%
CVS: Stopped selling tobacco products and quit the U.S. Chamber of Commerce to protest its pro-tobacco lobbying	23%	24%

Source: "Business and Politics: Do They Mix? Third Annual Study," Global Strategy Group, January 2016, https://globalstrategygroup.com/2016/01/27/gsgs-third-annual-study-business -politics-do-they-mix/.

Is it appropriate to take a stand? What consumers think

A Global Strategy Group survey showed that Americans tend to approve of corporate activism on economic issues more than activism on social issues.

Percentage of respondents who thought it was appropriate for companies to take a stance on each issue

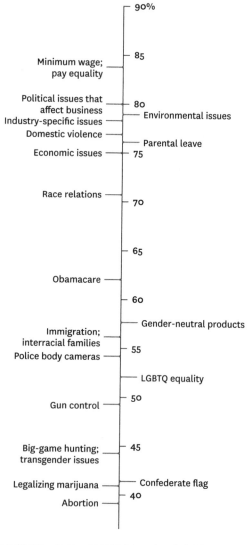

90%

85
Minimum wage; pay equality

Political issues that affect business — 80
Environmental issues
Industry-specific issues
Domestic violence
Parental leave
Economic issues — 75

Race relations — 70

65

Obamacare — 60

Gender-neutral products
Immigration; interracial families
55
Police body cameras
LGBTQ equality
Gun control — 50

Big-game hunting; transgender issues — 45

Legalizing marijuana — Confederate flag
Abortion — 40

Source: "Business and Politics: Do They Mix? Third Annual Study," Global Strategy Group, January 2016, https://globalstrategygroup.com/2016/01/27/gsgs-third-annual-study-business-politics-do-they-mix/.

ibility of business leaders rests on the perception that they make decisions after careful analysis, CEO activists can be effective only if they really understand the issue under debate.

When to weigh in

Once the issue is selected, the CEO activist has to understand if there are key moments when speaking out might actually make a difference. Is it while a piece of legislation is being considered, or is it afterward?

We have observed that a CEO activist's chances of blocking a particular policy are typically better than his or her chances of reversing legislation that has been enacted. As we have seen with the Republican Party's efforts to repeal the Affordable Care Act in recent months, the U.S. legislative system was designed to be slow moving and deliberative. This institutional feature makes it difficult not only to pass sweeping new legislation but to repeal existing laws as well.

Also, consider the news cycle. As we noted earlier, being the first CEO to quit one of the president's economic councils earned Frazier (and Merck) significant positive media coverage. When other CEOs quit in rapid succession over the next 48 hours, their stories were lumped together. Frazier's actions will likely be remembered more than those of the CEOs who followed him. Of course, there was a downside to all the attention: President Trump struck back directly at Frazier, tweeting an insult and citing Merck's responsibility for high drug prices. To date, there's no evidence that this has hurt Merck's business.

How to weigh in

CEO activism differs from traditional corporate engagement in politics precisely because it is visible and high profile. The CEO needs to decide whether he or she wants all that attention or if the cause would be better advanced by a coalition of CEOs. More than 160 CEOs and business leaders chose to sign a letter by the Human Rights Campaign opposing the North Carolina bathroom law. In taking this approach, they mitigated the risk of consumer backlash and amplified the newsworthiness and thus the impact of their activism. Collective action can also make it more difficult for critics to target

Implications for Democracy

CEO ACTIVISM MAY BE GIVING BUSINESSES and their leaders even more influence in a political system in which their money can already buy access to power. Some people, including North Carolina's lieutenant governor, who supported the bathroom bill while facing an onslaught of CEO activism, have gone further, characterizing it as corporate bullying. One Georgia state senator, who sponsored that state's religious freedom bill, lamented, "Marc Benioff is the ringleader for big-business CEOs who use economic threats to exercise more power over public policy than the voters who use the democratic process." From this perspective, CEO activism can be viewed as endangering democracy's ideal that each citizen should have an equal say in influencing policy outcomes.

There is of course another angle on this that considers CEO activism within the current environment of political influence. As we've noted, CEO activism is an unusually transparent way for corporate leaders to try to affect policy—in contrast to behind-the-scenes efforts to work with legislators, trade associations, and think tanks. Because CEO activism is highly visible, employees, customers, and the media can decide how to respond to it. There is also a political divide here. (To be sure, certain controversies transcend politics.) Some progressives have been appreciative of recent CEO activism while decrying the activities of business leaders like the Koch brothers. As a result, many conservatives see a double standard at play. Most of the CEO activists have been espousing liberal views, but it remains to be seen how widespread activism from conservative business leaders would be received.

---

individual corporate leaders and thus can be perceived as less risky. But it is slower by design and is likely to be less effective in associating a particular leader and corporate brand with a particular cause.

CEOs also may choose not to weigh in at all. Some leaders may feel that they do not understand the issue well enough, hold an unpopular view, or simply want to focus on other areas. All of those are credible reasons to hold back. But executives should expect that employees, the media, and other interested parties may ask why the CEO has not spoken out, and should be ready to explain the rationale.

The inside game

It's a good idea to make sure that internal stakeholders are aligned with CEO activism—or at least aware of it ahead of time. When Frazier was considering resigning from Trump's economic council, he reached out to his board members, who subsequently defended his decision and praised his courage and integrity. Our interviews suggest that not all CEOs consult with their directors or employees before taking public stands, which may imperil their efforts.

Though CEOs first have to decide whether they're speaking for themselves or their organizations, they should recognize that any statements they make will nonetheless be associated with their companies. We have seen almost no CEOs successfully separate themselves from their firms in this way. Given that, we advise setting up a rapid response team composed of representatives from the board, investors, senior management (including the chief communications officer), and employees to act as a kitchen cabinet on CEO activism. Seeking broad consensus across the organization could prevent CEO activism from being timely, which is often critical to attract attention to a message, but if the CEO can at least inform his or her cabinet about what to expect and why, it should greatly reduce the risk that key stakeholders will be unprepared for any backlash.

Predicting the reaction and gauging the results

CEO activists should prepare thoughtful responses to those who disagree with them. After Target modified its bathroom policy to accommodate transgender customers, hundreds of thousands of people signed a petition in protest. The literature tells us that when easy alternatives to a product or service are available, boycotts are more effective. Target is particularly vulnerable in this regard. Thus it's not surprising that the retail chain, which has many stores in politically conservative areas of the United States, has taken action to assuage the criticism by spending $20 million creating single-occupancy bathrooms in its stores. On the other hand, Nordstrom's customer base of affluent urban women did not threaten to abandon the upscale department store chain when President Trump attacked it for distancing itself from Ivanka Trump's apparel line.

Companies generally lack good data on the political beliefs of their customers, but this information would be useful in assessing potential reactions to CEO activism. CEOs and their companies are likely to know more about the political beliefs of their employees and can better predict their responses, however. Will employees rally to the cause or go public with their disapproval—as more than a thousand IBM employees did after CEO Virginia Rometty met with President Trump?

CEO activism also risks a backlash from politicians. Trump has tweeted his disagreement with numerous companies and their management decisions, marshaling millions of X/Twitter followers and creating public relations headaches. CEOs and their teams should be gaming out the likely response from supporters and critics in their own organizations, the media, and the political sphere.

It's imperative to hold postmortems, too, and answer the question: Did I make a difference? Metrics to assess the impact of activism should be established ahead of time, whether they be retweets, media mentions, public opinion polls, or actual policy shifts. Big swings in public opinion are rare, so it makes sense to set realistic goals, track intermediate outcomes, and measure progress over time.

CEO activism could become a first-order strategic issue. As more and more business leaders choose to speak out on contentious political and social matters, CEOs will increasingly be called on to help shape the debate about such issues. Many will decide to stay out of the fray, but they should still expect to be peppered with questions from employees, the media, and other stakeholders about the hot-button topics of day.

We believe CEOs need a playbook in this new world. To effectively engage in CEO activism, they should select issues carefully, reflect on the best times and approaches to get involved, consider the potential for backlash, and measure results. By following these guidelines, CEO activists can be more effective on the issues they care about most.

Originally published in January–February 2018. Reprint R1801E

Competing on Social Purpose

by Omar Rodríguez-Vilá and Sundar Bharadwaj

CONSUMERS INCREASINGLY EXPECT BRANDS to have not just functional benefits but a social purpose. As a result, companies are taking social stands in very visible ways. Airbnb used a Super Bowl ad to publicly cement its commitment to diversity. Tecate, based in Mexico, is investing heavily in programs to reduce violence against women, and Vicks, a P&G brand in India, supports child-adoption rights for transgender people. Brands increasingly use social purpose to guide marketing communications, inform product innovation, and steer investments toward social cause programs. And that's all well and good when it works. But missteps are common, and they can have real consequences.

Recall Starbucks's Race Together campaign—the chain's earnest effort to get customers talking about race relations in the United States. The program was widely criticized for its perceived lack of authenticity, among other reasons, and was quickly canceled. Or consider SunChips's 2010 launch of a biodegradable bag. The composite material was indeed good for the environment—but the bags were so noisy they drew mockery on social media, forcing the company to pull them from the market.

Countless well-intentioned social-purpose programs have consumed resources and management time only to end up in obscurity. Sometimes they backfire because the brand messages designed to promote them anger or offend customers—or they simply go unnoticed because they fail to resonate. Other times, managers use these initiatives solely to pursue intangible benefits such as brand affection or as a means to communicate the company's corporate social responsibility, without consideration of how they might create business value for the firm.

With the support of Sustainable Brands and the Ray C. Anderson Center for Sustainable Business, we've studied many social-purpose brand programs and have worked with close to a dozen leading brands to design growth-focused social-purpose strategies. On the basis of our research and experience, we've developed an approach we call "competing on social purpose" that ties a company's most ambitious social aspirations to its most pressing growth needs. In this article, we provide a novel framework to help companies find the right social purpose for their brands.

Building a Strategy

Some brands have integrated social purpose into their business models from the start: Think of Patagonia, TOMS, Warby Parker, and Seventh Generation. The societal benefit these "social purpose natives" offer is so deeply entwined with the product or service that it's hard to see the brands' surviving intact without it. Imagine how customers would react if TOMS abruptly ended its one-for-one program, which donates shoes, water, or eye care to the needy for every product it sells. And what would happen to Patagonia's brand if the company abandoned its commitment to eco-friendly manufacturing? Social purpose natives like these must be diligent stewards of their brands.

The challenges are very different for the much larger number of brands for which this article is written—a group we call "social-purpose immigrants." These established brands have grown without a well-defined social-purpose strategy and are now seeking to develop one. Typically, they belong to firms that are good corporate citizens and are committed to progress on environmental

Idea in Brief

The Expectation

Consumers increasingly expect brands to have a social purpose, so many companies are taking social stands in very visible ways. Think TOMS's one-for-one program, which donates shoes and other goods for every product sold.

The Challenge

These programs can benefit society and the brand but may fizzle or actually harm the company if they're not carefully managed.

The Strategy

An effective strategy creates value by strengthening a brand's key attributes or building new adjacencies. At the same time, it mitigates the risk of negative associations and threats to stakeholder acceptance.

and social goals. However, their growth has thus far been based on superior functional performance that is unrelated to a broader social purpose.

To develop a social purpose strategy, managers should begin by identifying a set of social or environmental needs to which the brand can make a meaningful contribution. (For simplicity, we'll use the term "social needs" to refer to both social and environmental concerns.) Few brands are likely to start with a blank slate—most have corporate social responsibility programs under way, some of which could become relevant aspects of the brand's value proposition. Yet focusing on only those initiatives could limit the potential of a purpose-driven brand strategy or divert marketing resources meant to stimulate the brand's growth toward corporate initiatives. To create a more comprehensive set of choices, managers should explore social purpose ideas in three domains: brand heritage, customer tensions, and product externalities.

Brand heritage

Of the many benefits a brand may confer, only a few are likely to have defined the brand from the start and be the core reason for its success. A look into the brand's heritage—the most salient benefits the brand offers customers—can help managers identify the social needs their brands are well positioned to address. For instance, since its launch in 1957, Dove has been promoted as a beauty bar, not a soap. Enhancing beauty has always been central to its value proposition. Therefore, it makes sense that Dove focuses on social needs tied to perceptions of beauty.

Customer tensions

An unbounded exploration of social issues relevant to your customer base will most likely yield a list that's too broad to be very helpful. To narrow your options, look at the "cultural tensions" that affect your customers and are related to your brand heritage. Such tensions, first characterized by marketing strategist Douglas Holt, refer to the conflict people often feel when their own experience conflicts with society's prevailing ideology. Holt argues that brands can become more relevant by addressing consumers' desire to resolve these tensions. Classic examples include Coca-Cola's "I'd Like to Teach the World to Sing" commercial, which promoted peace and unity at the height of the Vietnam War, and Budweiser's recent Super Bowl ad celebrating the immigrant story of one of its founders, which aired in the midst of a heated public debate about immigration.

Product externalities

Finally, examine your product's or industry's externalities—the indirect costs borne or benefits gained by a third party as a result of your products' manufacture or use. For instance, the food and beverage industry has been criticized for the contribution of some of its products to the increasing rates of childhood obesity. It has also faced concerns about negative health effects resulting from companies' use of artificial ingredients and other chemicals in their products. Panera Bread's decision to position its offerings as "clean food"— made without "artificial preservatives, sweeteners, flavors, or colors from artificial sources"—is a direct response to a social need created by industry externalities.

Obstacles to Competing on Purpose

THREE CHARACTERISTICS OF PURPOSE-DRIVEN growth make it particularly challenging for managers.

It's hard to change course. Once a social purpose is chosen, changing course is difficult and ill-advised, because success depends on the legitimacy of the brand's claim. Shifting or inconsistent claims may raise doubts about the firm's integrity or commitment. Specific programs can and should evolve, of course, and successful brands continually innovate. But the underlying purpose should remain constant. Dove has pursued its Real Beauty cause for more than a decade. Patagonia has advocated for environmental protection since its founding in 1973. Starbucks has consistently worked to promote social justice. Although an unswerving purpose is critical to success, this constraint can be frustrating to managers in an era characterized by agility and constant experimentation.

It's tough to gauge market potential. Proponents of social purpose initiatives often argue that the programs can help the business grow. And they can—but not without a carefully crafted strategy. Too often, strategies are based on projections of business impacts that are oversimplified or flawed. Even among customer segments that support a brand's social purpose, for example, individual consumers may take purpose into account to varying degrees when making product choices. In addition, the size of the customer segments inspired by a brand's social mission may vary significantly by product category, purchase occasion, and geography. Finally, data on the importance of societal benefits is often drawn from consumer surveys—as opposed to actual customer behavior—which may overstate true purchase intentions. Taken together, these factors can lead to unreliable estimates of market demand and growth.

It's easy to get distracted. Many purpose-driven brand initiatives have been launched with enthusiasm only to vanish without a ripple. One reason is that the appeal of "doing well by doing good" can distract managers from a brand's primary business needs. These nonstrategic programs can take on a life of their own, tempting managers to expand and dilute the focus of their brand purpose and split their attention in ways that don't help growth. Or, concerned about potential controversy, managers may distance the program from the brand's other business activities, giving rise to shell initiatives that have no real presence in the brand's value chain.

Although a company may build a sound social-purpose strategy that focuses on just one domain, ideally this exercise yields opportunities at the intersection of all three. Consider Airbnb's WeAccept social purpose strategy. The company's brand heritage is built on providing an open and inclusive platform, but in recent years concerns about race discrimination have once again risen to the forefront of cultural tension in the United States. Recently, Airbnb has faced allegations of racial discrimination by some of its members—a serious externality produced by its service.

Pare the List

After considering social purpose ideas in the three domains, managers should pare the list to three or four social needs, and propose strategies for each, to be evaluated as final candidates for the brand's social purpose.

To guide the prioritization and selection process, managers should gauge how the social purpose idea both generates business value and minimizes the company's exposure to risk. An effective social-purpose strategy creates value by strengthening a brand's key attributes or building new adjacencies. At the same time, it mitigates the risk of negative associations among consumers and threats to stakeholder acceptance.

Brand attributes

Managers often consider the fit between the social need and the brand as a criterion for evaluating social purpose strategies. However, good fit isn't enough. They should also consider how social purpose can create value by strengthening (or creating) brand attributes relevant to consumer choice in a given industry.

We define brand attributes as characteristics managers instill in a product or service, including features and benefits as well as personality or reputation supported through marketing communications. A restaurant, for example, might use sustainably sourced ingredients (a feature), which can reinforce a perception of great taste (a benefit), and through marketing communications, promote a reputation for environmental consciousness (the brand personality).

When choosing among possible social-purpose strategies, managers need to understand how each option affects key brand attributes. Consider the case of Vaseline. By 2014, when Kathleen Dunlop became global brand director, the product was at risk of becoming a commodity in the United States. To grow, it needed to find new ways to remind existing customers of its core attributes while educating a younger generation.

Dunlop and her team determined that the answer to this business problem lay in the brand's tagline "the healing power of Vaseline," which captures its core attribute. Asking "Where is our healing power most urgently needed?" the team began the process of developing a social purpose strategy for the brand. Through interviews with medical professionals at the Centers for Disease Control, Doctors Without Borders, and the UN Refugee Agency, the team learned that Vaseline jelly was an indispensable part of emergency first-aid kits. In refugee camps, for instance, minor but common skin conditions such as cracking and blistering could become dangerous and debilitating. Petroleum jelly, and Vaseline in particular, was often a first line of care.

With this insight, the team crystallized a social purpose strategy around skin care for the most vulnerable—people living in poverty or emergency conditions—and in 2015 the Vaseline Healing Project was born. In partnership with the nonprofit Direct Relief, the project aims to reach 5 million people by 2020.

The Healing Project was not a CSR or public relations initiative; it was designed to connect business goals with societal needs. The resulting campaign was tested alongside other traditional marketing programs designed to differentiate the brand. The initiative outperformed all the alternatives and achieved its objectives in its first full year, helping Dunlop build a stronger business case for it and persuade the managers responsible for the brand's P&L to invest marketing resources behind it. Now in its third year and with more than 2.3 million jars of Vaseline donated, the initiative is continuing to expand.

The Social Benefit Pyramid

MANAGERS OFTEN STRUGGLE TO RECONCILE corporate-level sustainability efforts, CSR programs, and social purpose strategies for their brands, causing them to misdirect brand marketing resources toward increasing consumer awareness of corporate-wide programs.

To ensure the proper allocation of resources, brand managers should clarify the roles of existing or potential social initiatives for the brand. First, sort the initiatives into "front-end" investments (those the brand will actively promote to customers), "back-end" investments (those that the company practices but that do not create value for consumers), and activities the brand won't pursue at all. Then, select one social purpose initiative to compete on and several to "claim" in brand marketing. All others should not be an active part of the brand's marketing efforts.

The chart below shows how this categorization would work for the Dove brand.

A closer look: Dove brand

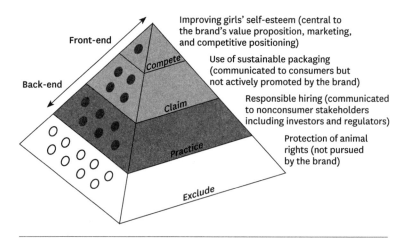

Front-end

Back-end

Compete — Improving girls' self-esteem (central to the brand's value proposition, marketing, and competitive positioning)

Use of sustainable packaging (communicated to consumers but not actively promoted by the brand)

Claim — Responsible hiring (communicated to nonconsumer stakeholders including investors and regulators)

Practice — Protection of animal rights (not pursued by the brand)

Exclude

To assess the relationship between different social-purpose strategies and brand attributes, managers should ask:

- Does the strategy reinforce existing brand attributes?

- What new and valuable brand attributes might it create?

- Would the strategy be difficult for competitors to imitate?

Business adjacencies

One reason a brand purpose strategy can fall short of expectations is that it doesn't adequately address the financial interests of investors and other stakeholders. One way a social purpose strategy can boost business performance is by enabling the brand to compete in adjacent markets.

Consider Brita, which until 2005 primarily sold tap-water filters. Concerned by slowing growth, managers realized that the company could enter the adjacent bottled-water market by positioning filtered water as an environmentally friendly alternative. Thus Brita seized on a social need-waste reduction—to push into a new market. It combined reusable water-bottle and pitcher innovations with its filter technology to expand the brand's market presence. In its marketing, Brita emphasized the water's "great taste and purity" and its economic value over time relative to bottled water. But its central message was the environmental benefit of substituting filtered water for bottled water: 300 plastic bottles kept out of landfills and oceans for each Brita filter used.

Most recently, the brand has evolved its strategy by positioning itself as not just a filter brand but also a water brand, promoting additional social benefits related to health and wellness. This strategy helped Brita secure a strong competitive position: It was relatively straightforward for the brand to enter the bottled water category, but it would be much harder for bottled water rivals to enter the filter business. Three years after Brita entered this adjacent market, its revenues had grown by 47%.

To gauge whether a proposed brand purpose and strategy can support a move into adjacent markets, managers should ask:

- Can the strategy help create a new product or service for current customers?

- Can it help open a new market or channel or attract a new customer segment?

- Can it help reduce costs or increase the profitability of the business?

Consumer associations

It's important to think through how consumers will perceive the social purpose a brand is considering. Will they see the benefits as an asset? A liability? Or irrelevant to their purchase decision? In predicting customer response, brand managers need to understand the range of cognitive associations that different consumer segments may bring to a brand's social claim. Take, for instance, the brand attribute "organic ingredients," which is typically used to support claims of health or environmental benefits. If it appears on the label of a tea product, consumers may associate it with augmented qualities—perhaps improved taste or healthfulness. But how might they react to an organic dry-cleaning service? A growing body of research demonstrates that consumers don't have an equal or easily predictable response to social benefit claims: Labels like "fair trade," "environmentally friendly," and "ethically sourced" can sometimes induce negative associations—such as poorer performance, in the case of the dry cleaner.

Consider the Green Works line of environmentally friendly cleaning products. Launched with high expectations by Clorox in 2008, the brand has failed to generate the anticipated sales and the company's plans to become the dominant player in this premium market have yet to become reality. Before launching Green Works, Clorox's market research revealed that although consumers expressed interest in "green" cleaning products, only a small minority (15%) perceived environmentally friendly ingredients as an important consideration in their purchase decisions. The research also showed that mainstream consumers often associated environmental friendliness with diminished performance. Clorox product managers delayed the product launch twice until they were confident their formulation was as effective as traditional cleaners. In addition, they decided to include the Clorox logo on the label to reinforce the message of cleaning efficacy.

Despite these efforts, Green Works ran into problems. Eco-conscious consumers who might have been attracted to Green Works' environmental credentials were put off by its association with Clorox—an industrial-strength cleaner that they did not perceive as environmentally friendly—while mainstream consumers remained unconvinced that the products were effective enough. In response, the company revamped the packaging to satisfy both groups: The Clorox logo has disappeared, and messages about powerful cleaning are now prominent on the label. Green Works' experience demonstrates the importance of carefully evaluating the associations—both positive and negative—that consumers may bring to each social-benefit claim a brand makes.

To assess the associations consumers may have with different brand-purpose strategies, managers should consider the following questions:

- Is the social need likely to be perceived as personally relevant to target consumers?

- Will consumers be able to easily associate the brand with the social purpose?

- Will the social purpose strategy induce positive (and not negative) associations about the brand or product?

Stakeholder acceptance

Competing on social purpose is sure to attract criticism—virtually all social issues have both advocates and detractors—which can stall or even derail a program. Thus, managers must evaluate whether key stakeholders will accept and support the proposed social-purpose strategy. As with customer associations, some stakeholders may embrace a brand purpose while others reject it. Our research has found three drivers of negative reactions: inconsistency between the brand claim and the company's actions, politicization of the claim, and suspicion about the firm's motives.

Consider again Dove brand's Campaign for Real Beauty. The marketing program challenged traditional standards of beauty and promoted the idea that true beauty has limitless forms. Its success made the brand a leading example of how to effectively integrate a social purpose into an existing brand strategy. But as its popularity grew, the campaign also attracted criticism. Some detractors noted an inconsistency between Dove's position and those of its parent company Unilever, particularly in the marketing of the Axe line of men's grooming products, whose advertising featured the seduction of scantily clad women. That Unilever was simultaneously fighting and reinforcing stereotypical notions of beauty struck its critics as hypocritical. Unilever eventually repositioned Axe and removed sexist stereotypes from its marketing. When competing on social purpose, inconsistencies between your operations and your brand claims will become more salient and should be quickly resolved—or, better, avoided in the first place.

Another obstacle to stakeholder acceptance occurs when companies, unwittingly or not, adopt a controversial social purpose. This was the case with Coca-Cola's Arctic Home program, a partnership launched in 2011 with the World Wildlife Fund to protect polar bears. The social mission fit well with the brand, which had long used the animal in its advertising. However, despite the fact that its leaders never intended to equate a conservation initiative with the politics of climate change, the program catapulted Coke into the middle of a political debate. A significant segment of the population regarded global warming as a serious problem. But climate skeptics saw the Coke campaign as a mass media effort to promote a political agenda. Coke's program was interpreted by some as a position on climate change and became a talking point in a Senate debate. As a result, some retail customers refused to use the campaign in their stores. While the company succeeded in containing a more general outcry, its experience highlights the risk of politicization around a brand's social purpose. It is unlikely that any social-benefit claim can escape criticism, but management's goal must be to maximize the fan-to-foe ratio.

Finally, stakeholders may question a brand's motives if the initiative appears to be driven primarily by commercial interests. Stakeholders understand that companies are profit-driven, but if the company's initiative offers no apparent social benefit, they may feel manipulated—as often happens if a brand is found to be "greenwashing." To mitigate this risk, it's critical to select a social purpose for which the brand can make a material contribution.

To assess whether the social purpose strategy is likely to be accepted by stakeholders, managers should ask:

- Can the brand have a demonstrable impact on the social need?

- Are key stakeholders on the front lines of the social issue likely to support the brand actions?

- Can the brand avoid inconsistent messaging, perception of opportunism, and politicization?

Nike: A Case Study

Let's look at how our framework can be applied in practice. Although numerous brands are using this method to evaluate brand purpose strategies, their initiatives are still under way. For illustrative purposes, we've analyzed the choices made by Nike over the past several decades. (For more, see the sidebar "Gauging Social Purpose Strategies.")

Over the past decade, Nike has invested heavily in R&D to reduce environmental waste in its manufacturing processes. In 2010, the company launched the Environmental Apparel Design software tool—an open-source version of its Considered Design Index—enabling garment designers anywhere to assess the environmental

Gauging Social Purpose Strategies

TO COMPARE BRAND PURPOSE STRATEGIES, score each option on its potential to create value or reduce risk by answering the questions below. Strategies that score highest across domains are the most likely to create value for the company and effectively address the targeted social need. Below, we assess how two options for Nike would stack up.

Nike: Scoring two options

Answer the questions below, giving one point for each "yes" answer

	Decreasing material waste in manufacturing	Promoting the participation of girls in sports
Brand Attributes		
Does the strategy reinforce existing brand attributes?	0	1
Will it create new brand attributes?	1	1
Will it be difficult for competitors to imitate?	0	0
Total score	**1**	**2**
Business Adjacencies		
Will the strategy help create a new product or service for current customers?	0	1
Will it help open a new market or distribution channel?	1	1
Will it help reduce costs or increase the profitability of the business?	1	0
Total score	**2**	**2**
Consumer Associations		
Is the social need likely to be perceived as personally relevant to target consumers?	0	1
Will consumers easily see the connection between the brand and the social need?	0	1
Will the strategy induce positive associations about the brand?	0	1
Total score	**0**	**3**

Stakeholder Acceptance

Can the brand have a demonstrable impact on the social need?	1	1
Will key stakeholders on the front lines of the issue support the strategy?	1	1
Can the brand avoid inconsistent messaging, perceptions of opportunism, and politicization?	1	1
Total score	**3**	**3**

Plotting the scores for Nike's two options on a spider chart clearly demonstrates that promoting the participation of girls in sports creates more value for the brand and mitigates risk better than decreasing material waste in manufacturing would.

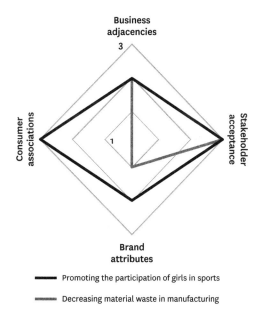

impact of various materials and explore combinations that reduce material waste before making a selection. In 2012, Nike debuted its flyknit technology, which allows the company to reduce waste by manufacturing shoes with a one-piece upper body.

Nike could tout these efforts in its customer-facing marketing, but it doesn't. In their purchase decisions, customers look for performance shoes that are comfortable, lightweight, and durable. Reducing manufacturing waste is not an attribute most sports-shoe buyers prioritize. Claims of environmental friendliness are also unlikely to help the brand move into adjacent markets. In fact, people buying performance shoes are more likely to associate green-manufacturing claims with reduced durability. Nike does communicate its environmental benefits to partners and investors—for whom these are important operating practices—demonstrating a wise allocation of its social benefit claims.

In 1995 Nike embraced a customer-facing social benefit: encouraging young girls to participate in sports. Nike spokeswoman Vizhier Corpus said at the time, "If you are a parent interested in raising a girl who is physically and emotionally strong, then look to sports as a means to that end." It was a smart choice. The message reinforced the brand associations of courage and competition promoted by Nike in the 1990s, was unlikely to suffer from problems with stakeholder acceptance, and had a robust business logic: At the time, the women's apparel business represented less than 10% of Nike's revenues. Today that figure has climbed to 23%, and women's apparel is the company's highest growth segment.

Define the Brand's Role

Once a company decides which social need a brand will focus on, using the four dimensions of our framework to guide their selection, managers must determine how the brand strategy will create value for it. Our analysis of dozens of purpose-driven brand strategies revealed four ways a brand can create value for a social need. This taxonomy provides a useful tool for thinking about how a brand can best execute on its purpose. It can also guide managers in the selection of metrics for measuring the impact of their social-purpose investments.

1. Generate resources
Brands can make an impact by helping generate the resources required to address a social need. Most commonly, this involves the donation of financial resources: When consumers buy a product, the brand gives a percentage of the profits to a selected cause. Newman's Own famously donates 100% of profits across thousands of organizations that address four broad social needs. Resources could also include, time, talent, relationships, and capabilities.

2. Provide choices
Brands can offer consumers products that address a social need and can be substituted for those that don't. Brita filters, for example, give customers an alternative to bottled water that doesn't add plastic to landfills.

3. Influence mindsets
Brands can help shift perspectives on social issues. Examples include Nike's communications efforts to promote the participation of girls in sports and its recent campaign to promote racial and gender equality. Other examples include Tecate's initiative to stop gender violence in Mexico or the Always brand's "Like a Girl" program that focused on building girls' self-esteem.

4. Improve conditions
Brand actions can help establish the conditions necessary to address a social need. Consider Coca-Cola's Ekocenter initiative in Africa. Through a multi-stakeholder partnership, the brand is creating community centers with clean water, solar power, and internet access, among other services. The centers house modular markets run by local female entrepreneurs.

In defining how their social purpose programs will create value, managers should partner with organizations and individuals that are actively working on the front lines of the social issue. This ensures that the brand's capabilities are focused on the most pressing needs of the social issue.

Managers often have the best intentions when trying to link their brands with a social need, but choosing the right one can be difficult and risky and has long-term implications. Competing on social purpose requires managers to create value for all stakeholders—customers, the company, shareholders, and society at large—merging strategic acts of generosity with the diligent pursuit of brand goals.

Originally published in September–October 2017. Reprint R1705G

The Messy but Essential Pursuit of Purpose

by Ranjay Gulati

AS PURPOSE-DRIVEN STARTUPS GO, Gotham Greens is a tremendous success story. The company uses advanced hydroponic farming techniques to grow fresh, high-quality, pesticide-free produce, which it now sells in more than 40 U.S. states. Since its launch in 2009, it has redeveloped 500,000 square feet of out-of-use city industrial spaces and brownfield sites into modern urban greenhouses—facilities that use 95% less water and 97% less land than conventional farms do. Profitable since its first year, it's been named one of *Business Insider*'s "50 Coolest New Businesses in America." By the close of 2020 the company had attracted $130 million in investment.

Gotham Greens clearly delivers social and environmental benefits, making good on its mission of finding new ways to produce local food, revitalize communities, and innovate for a sustainable future. At the same time, it's creating wealth for its employees and investors. It's an example of what my Harvard Business School colleague Michael Porter and the FSG cofounder Mark Kramer have dubbed "shared value" and what Whole Foods Market's CEO, John Mackey, calls "conscious capitalism."

And yet not even Gotham Greens always realizes its ideals perfectly. If you've bought its produce, you know that the greens come in single-use plastic packaging, which is terrible for the environment. Why would a company so dedicated to sustainable, low-waste production make such a decision? As its CEO, Viraj Puri, has explained, it was a difficult but well-researched, mindfully made, and necessary trade-off—the kind that even the most noble companies must constantly make to truly deliver long-term value for all stakeholders.

Over the past three years I've conducted in-depth research on how mission-driven organizations—both old and young and spanning a variety of industries and geographies—succeed. No question, the best of them strive to deliver on their purpose while also generating profits at every turn. Indeed, they see purpose in the same light as profit—as a generative force that expands and improves everything about an organization. For example, you might see a manufacturing company shifting to new energy sources that pollute less and reduce costs, or a bank hiring a more diverse workforce, which benefits the community, brings the bank closer to its customer base, and spurs revenue-generating innovation.

However, smart corporate leaders understand that such win-win solutions—those that yield universal short-term benefits—often aren't possible. How can a company move forward when it can't simultaneously achieve purpose and profit? When it's impossible to satisfy different groups of stakeholders in equal measure at the same time?

Many companies revert to a profit-first strategy when the going gets tough. Others, more committed to their mission, might cling to it instead, come hell or high water—or bankruptcy. But if your end goal is to create long-term value and have a meaningful positive impact on the world, neither of those strategies is tenable.

My research, conducted at an array of large public and private companies, points to a better approach. It involves using purpose as a North Star to clarify priorities and inspire action in situations where trade-offs must be made. It requires leaders to lean into such deliberations in consultation with stakeholders; to look beyond short-term, win-win solutions for ones that are good enough for now and promise broader benefits in the future; and finally, to effectively communicate the thinking behind those difficult decisions to garner support.

Idea in Brief

Most forward-thinking executives have embraced the notion that purpose-driven companies can solve social and environmental problems while also generating wealth, creating win-win outcomes that benefit everyone. But ideal solutions are rare. Many purpose-driven companies revert to a profit-first strategy if the going gets tough. Others doggedly pursue purpose but then find that their businesses are unsustainable. Using case studies on Etsy, Livongo, and other diverse companies, the author offers practical examples that leaders can use to think creatively about how to deliver as much benefit as possible to all their stakeholders.

This isn't an easy process. In fact, it can be excruciatingly difficult. But evidence from dozens of companies—including Gotham Greens, the personal-health-care company Livongo, the handmade-goods marketplace Etsy, the HR-technology conglomerate Recruit, the diversified industrials multinational Mahindra Group, and the plant and advanced-materials-engineering company Bühler—shows that it works.

Pursuing Deep Purpose

Before we dig into the messy but critical process of successfully navigating tradeoffs, let me describe what I define as a *deep purpose* company.

In my work studying and advising organizations over the past few decades, I've reviewed hundreds of purpose and mission statements and found that the most compelling—and most effective in guiding decision-making—have two basic and interrelated features. First, they delineate an ambitious long-term goal for the organization. Second, they give that goal an idealistic cast, committing to the fulfillment of broader social duties. These statements are meant to assert the commercial and societal problems a business intends to profitably solve for its stakeholders. They succinctly communicate what a company is all about and who it hopes to benefit.

Deep purpose companies thoroughly embed their purpose in their strategy, processes, communications, human resources practices, operational decision-making, and even culture. Sadly, such enterprises are quite limited in number. The vast majority of companies practice what I call *convenient purpose:* They talk about purpose but act on it only in superficial ways.

Some set out high-minded goals and serve society to an extent while continuing to sell products and services that cause serious harm. Depending on your moral perspective, certain companies dealing in fossil fuels, tobacco, alcohol, junk food, and weapons, and even some traditional and social media, fall into this category. Their commitment to social good isn't strong or broad enough to lead them to divest from lucrative but questionable businesses. This is *purpose as a disguise.* At an extreme, companies may even use lofty missions to hide malfeasance. Examples include Theranos, the blood-testing startup that promised a pathway to personalized health care but is said to have faked the efficacy of its equipment, and Purdue Pharma, which allegedly pumped sales of its breakthrough pain-relief medication OxyContin so dramatically that the result was a devastating opioid epidemic.

Other organizations offer what I call *purpose on the periphery:* They work to do good through corporate social responsibility (CSR) efforts and to do well through their core businesses, but they keep the two separate. While helping society to a degree and certainly rewarding shareholders, they stop short of transforming themselves into entities that promote environmental sustainability, community support, and employee well-being.

Then there are the *purpose as a win-win* companies. They aim for the sweet spot where social and economic value intersect. However, they tend to deliver only when ideal outcomes are possible (which is less often than one might think) and thus typically fail on either profit or purpose measures—more often on the latter. As the journalist and commentator Anand Giridharadas has argued, the "promise of painlessness"—the idea that "what is good for me will be good for you" and that investors and top executives need not sacrifice for the public good—is terribly naive.

Deep purpose organizations are different. As the name indicates, they are deeply committed to both positive social and positive commercial outcomes, framing even the smallest decisions, actions, and processes with their goals and duties in mind. Their leaders adopt a mindset of practical idealism. That means they don't simply accept trade-offs—they immerse themselves in them. They are determined to bring their corporate purpose to life, but they also understand that they must play and win within the constraints of our capitalist system.

Weighing purpose and profit in decision-making

Leaders may be motivated by social factors (the environment, communities, employees, suppliers, customers) or commercial factors (primarily shareholder interests and, sometimes indirectly, customers, employees, and suppliers) in their decision-making. Decisions that fall into the top right quadrant drive both, even if some trade-offs come into play. Those in the lower left quadrant do little good for anyone. The upper left and lower right quadrants represent choices that benefit either shareholders or society but not both.

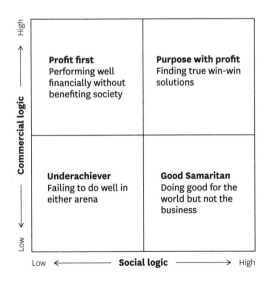

Consider the exhibit "Weighing purpose and profit in decision-making." Every purpose-driven, for-profit company claims to be aiming for the "purpose with profit" box. Deep purpose businesses, with leaders who embrace practical idealism, get there more often than others because they are not only truly committed to purpose with profit but also willing to reside in the "profit first" or the "Good Samaritan" quadrant for a time, provided they see a way to move over or up to the win-win ideal in the future. They may avoid decisions that yield only commercial gain with no prospect of social benefit. But if a choice boosts profit in a way that will one day do widespread good, they may make it and work hard to ensure that it eventually provides multistakeholder benefits. Likewise, if they have a Good Samaritan idea that they believe will become profitable over time, they may take a risk on it and then do everything possible to ensure that it works financially.

These leaders recognize the impossibility of devising perfect solutions that benefit all parties equally all the time. They settle instead on arrangements that may require a short-term or partial sacrifice by some but generate a balance of long-term value for everyone.

Making Tough Choices

Now let's examine how companies and leaders successfully manage these trade-offs.

By stubbornly fixing on purpose as a North Star

According to Puri at Gotham Greens, a commitment to environmental stewardship (in tandem with corporate growth) permeates the company's "entire DNA." That means it's the starting point for any decision-making, whether executives are framing long-term strategy or addressing small-scale tactical questions.

Take the packaging dilemma. After researching various eco-friendly options, Puri's team first chose highly attractive, compostable fiber containers. Affordable and good for the environment, they seemed like an exciting win-win. But as workers began harvesting and packaging lettuce, the company encountered a problem: The greens lasted only a few days before wilting, compared with two weeks or longer in plastic.

From there the company could have gone the Good Samaritan route, sticking with the compostable fiber and in due time possibly going out of business as retailers and consumers rejected the less-than-crisp greens. Or it could have quickly opted for profit and switched to plastic without a second thought. Instead, guided by its mission, it embarked on several more months of research.

One alternative was to leave the produce unpackaged, with supermarkets selling to consumers in loose bins. But shoppers had been gravitating away from such purchases, perceiving packaged greens to be cleaner, of higher quality, and safer to eat. Retail buyers said they might still order from Gotham Greens, but not nearly as much as they'd planned to. That was no recipe for an enterprise to succeed in its larger vision of reinventing agriculture.

Next Puri and his team researched various types of plastic, again with sustainability as their primary focus. Recyclable and recycled plastic intrigued them, but it would be too costly. Compostable plastic seemed most promising, but the team soon concluded that it wasn't as "green" as it seemed, because suppliers used subsidized, genetically modified corn to manufacture it, and only consumers who lived near the right municipal facilities could compost it. Most of it would wind up in landfills or, worse, mixed in with recyclables when it didn't qualify.

In the end Gotham Greens decided on #1 PET plastic, the most universally accepted at recycling facilities. Ten years later it's still using the same boxes. But it also has a dedicated group of employees who stay abreast of new technologies and search for more-sustainable options. Purpose in this instance was not only the starting point for decision-making but also a constant source of clarity that helped leaders sharpen their evolving understanding of a difficult trade-off and make informed and deliberate choices to navigate it.

Livongo is another organization that has used purpose as its North Star in making difficult decisions. Glen Tullman founded the company in 2014 with a simple but revolutionary mission: to help people with chronic conditions such as diabetes, which requires regular blood-glucose monitoring, stay healthy without constant visits to hospitals or doctors' offices. This was a personal cause for Tullman, a serial health-care entrepreneur: A decade earlier his son Sam, then age eight, had been diagnosed with type 1 diabetes.

Livongo—short for "Live Life on the Go"—equips users ("members" in its parlance) with devices that provide immediate health metrics after glucose test strips are inserted and then upload the data to the cloud, allowing consistent tracking, interpretation, recommendations, and even alerts when data looks off. With their mission of making members' lives easier always at the forefront, Tullman and his team made some unconventional trade-offs early on.

These included giving away glucose test strips as a way of getting people to use them more often; hiring a virtual care team to provide real-time advice in emergency situations; and keeping individuals on the platform even if they left the employers that initially enabled their subscription to the service. All represented big investments for a small startup—Good Samaritan decisions at the time—but Livongo knew that a long-term payoff would come in the form of customer retention and value creation for investors. Within two years of its launch, the company had 53,000 active members across more than 200 clients, 100 employees with soaring engagement rates, and close to $40 million in revenue. Following its IPO in July 2019, Livongo was valued at $3.4 billion. Last year, before its merger with Teladoc, the company was valued at $18.5 billion.

By leaning in to trade-offs

Deep purpose companies and their leaders resist the urge to dodge tough decisions. Instead they are willing to linger in a space of discomfort, ambiguity, and contradiction. That's why Gotham Greens spent months investigating the best kind of packaging and ultimately settled for an imperfect solution while continuing to look for a better one.

As Sarah Kaplan of the Rotman School has remarked, companies don't get ahead by "declaring the problems irresolvable." They must learn to "persevere until they reconcile those tensions." Doing that should involve intense consultation with stakeholders to gain insight into their perspectives, the implications various decisions might have for them, and which moves they regard as deal-breakers. Consider how Puri's team talked to retail buyers, engaged materials and recycling experts, and involved its own employees throughout its decision-making process.

Etsy, the online arts-and-crafts marketplace, has leaned into even higher-stakes trade-offs in recent years. Founded in 2005 by the craftsman Rob Kalin and three others, the company has always been defined by its purpose of giving "makers" a venue and tools for marketing their wares and creating their own small businesses. By 2012, under a new CEO, Chad Dickerson, Etsy had adopted a more ambitious mission—"to reimagine commerce in ways that build a more fulfilling and lasting world"—and become a certified B Corporation, a designation given to companies that meet strict environmental, social, and governance standards. By 2015, the year it went public, it was facilitating $2 billion in sales for some 1.4 million sellers each year and attracting top talent thanks to its social purpose and generous workplace policies. What Etsy wasn't delivering was profit: It had lost money since 2012, and within nine months of that IPO, investors had lost patience. The stock plunged 75%, Dickerson was fired, and in 2017 a new CEO, Josh Silverman, was appointed.

Silverman understood the assignment: His job was to rethink how Etsy could better operate to everyone's benefit, rebalancing among stakeholders and injecting more accountability into both its commercial and its social efforts. As he and his team worked to diagnose the problems, they realized that the company had been prioritizing employee and broader societal concerns (key requirements of B Corp certification) over sellers and shareholders, which was a big threat to its long-term health.

Over the next few months Etsy made some major changes: It laid off 160 employees (on top of the 80 it had let go before Silverman's arrival), which amounted to about a quarter of its workforce; shut down projects that were staff favorites; disbanded its existing sustainability group; and announced that it would let its B Corp certification lapse. The blowback was harsh. One disgruntled former employee described those moves as "a cautionary tale of capitalism."

And yet, as Silverman described it to me, he was playing the long game, keeping Etsy's purpose and all its stakeholders in mind. Within a few years the company was able to hire again, and its impact initiatives (refined to focus on three key areas: empowering people, environmental responsibility, and diversity) began to bear fruit. Silverman estimates that the trade-offs the company made in 2017 have allowed it to become five times as productive, as measured by the number of weekly software releases its engineers churn out to improve the selling and buying experience on the site.

Gross sales climbed in each of the past three years, and Etsy has been profitable since 2017. In 2020, thanks to a surge in pandemic sales, its sellers numbered more than 4 million, and they generated more than $1.7 billion in revenue and $349 million in net income for the company. It currently employs about 1,400 people, a few hundred more than it did before the layoffs. And social impact in its key areas is also impressive: Etsy has contributed about $6 billion to the maker economy; it is the first major online shopping destination to offset 100% of emissions from shipping; and it has doubled the number of underrepresented minorities on its staff and has a majority female workforce. As it has done all this, its stock price has shot up.

By looking beyond short-term win-wins to accept good-enough-for-now solutions that will lead to broader long-term benefits
Practical idealism means refusing to sacrifice real, albeit incomplete, progress in the name of perfection and being brave enough to take future-focused action that might cause short-term pain for some. Without question, that happened at Etsy. Livongo's decisions weren't immediately beneficial to investors. Gotham Greens' use of plastic has a negative impact on the environment.

Remember, though, that even imperfect decisions must be made thoughtfully, with an eye to achieving your social objectives *and* profit someday soon. When a business idea or a course of action would primarily create social value, recognize that you might want to take the leap before commercial value seems entirely attainable, but continue to aggressively explore options and give yourself a timeline. When potential plans would primarily drive commercial value, investigate ways they might help you deliver social impact as well, and if those projections are positive, continue. (If they're not, disengage.) In a legacy business you can try to graft purpose onto your existing products, services, and initiatives—for instance, by making your operations more sustainable and socially responsible or your products safer or healthier. Or you can take a portfolio approach, supplementing your efforts with others that better serve all stakeholders while also taking the steps and making the investments needed to shift your business from purpose on the periphery to deep purpose as soon as possible.

At Recruit, the Japan-based company that owns job-focused websites such as Indeed and Glassdoor along with staffing, recruitment, and HR technology businesses around the world, management would "never, ever" fund a project that delivered only financial returns, its former CHRO Shogo Ikeuchi told me, because that would violate one of its three core principles: "Prioritize social value." (The others are "Wow the world" and "Bet on passion.") At the same time, he insisted, the company wouldn't support projects that serve society but lack commercial potential. "Always, always we have borne in mind the balance between social value and economics," he said.

As of 2020 Recruit has for eight years funded one of its Japan-based ventures, Study Sapuri, an online learning plat form for students that is designed to address the country's educational inequities, in the hope of making it profitable. But this is not passive patience. Executives are constantly having "heated debate, discussion on how we can grow this business . . . how can we possibly generate more revenue?" Ikeuchi explained.

A similar story comes from Mahindra Group's farming equipment business, which decided to make its farming-as-a-service (FaaS) technology available free. That ate into profits but was a way to quickly and efficiently serve the broader company's mission—to "innovatively use all our resources to drive positive change in the lives of our stakeholders and communities across the world" (or, in the company's shorthand, just "Rise"). Cash-poor farmers got immediate access to state-of-the-art tech that would increase their productivity and boost their income potential. The eventual financial benefits were also in sight, however: Free FaaS helped the company gain market share and strengthened its business.

By effectively communicating the rationale

When making trade-offs, it's critical to explain the logic behind your decisions so that stakeholders understand how they connect to and support purpose. Being explicit builds trust and cohesion by giving meaning to the sacrifices some stakeholders are making and reinforcing a mutual commitment to shared long-term benefits.

Leaders at Etsy were quite explicit with employees and customers in explaining why the 2017 restructuring was necessary to put the company back on a sound financial footing and deliver on its promise to create the best maker marketplace in the world. Silverman and others speak openly about the sometimes imperfect decisions they came to. Livongo, Recruit, and Mahindra never hid their purpose-driven choices from shareholders (which were venture capitalists for Livongo and public market investors for the other two); instead executives outlined exactly why they were making those choices and how they would ultimately lead to better returns.

Bühler, a fifth-generation family-owned business that specializes in high-end milling, grinding, sorting, and die-casting machines and process engineering and services expertise, is constantly working to justify its pursuit of strict sustainability standards to its customers and its private owners. Some customers buy in, but others are more skeptical, worrying that the company is sacrificing performance for social goals. A few even feel that its reps and executives have become overly moralistic, "lecturing" them about how to run their businesses. As an employee at one large client told me, "No one is going to say, 'Oh, great, it's a perfectly sustainable company, so I'll just spend more" with it than would be necessary with a competitor.

As a result, Bühler needs to be extremely careful when courting new business, its former HR chief Dipak Mane told me. At the start of a bidding process, its reps tend to focus on "hard" dimensions such as quality, longevity, and price. But once they've progressed to later rounds, they transition to a greater emphasis on purpose, which they believe distinguishes the company from competitors whose product or service specs are otherwise equivalent. The chance to be a part of "saving the world" helps customers justify their choice of Bühler. The company's CEO, Stefan Scheiber, summed it up well: "What's the value? If I cannot answer that, then it's not good."

Acting with Intention in an Imperfect World

To drive performance and inspire stakeholders, leaders must abandon the notion that win-win solutions are the only ones that count. Of course, you should avoid underachiever decisions at all costs. And you shouldn't content yourself with just doing good or just racking up profit—you must constantly challenge yourself to do both. But recognize that you won't get it perfectly right for everyone all the time and that sometimes the best way to arrive at broad long-term benefits is to patiently negotiate short-term sacrifices.

Ultimately, the purity of your intention is what counts, along with the ferocity with which you pursue and manifest it. Stakeholders know that you can't perfectly align their interests every time. But their commitment to the company and its purpose deepens when you consistently make a valiant and thoughtful effort. You can make purpose meaningful in your organization by approaching every choice determined to serve all stakeholders to the greatest extent possible but mindful that trade-offs are sometimes absolutely necessary.

When deep purpose leaders bend idealism's arc to accommodate the practicalities of commerce, and vice versa, they ultimately generate more widely shared value. They also show us all what we can accomplish if we don't push our ideals to the extreme but instead seek to realize them in measured, practical, and sustainable ways.

Originally published in March–April 2022. Reprint S22022

From Purpose to Impact

by Nick Craig and Scott Snook

The two most important days in your life are the day you are born and the day you find out why.

—Mark Twain

OVER THE PAST FIVE YEARS, there's been an explosion of interest in purpose-driven leadership. Academics argue persuasively that an executive's most important role is to be a steward of the organization's purpose. Business experts make the case that purpose is a key to exceptional performance, while psychologists describe it as the pathway to greater well-being.

Doctors have even found that people with purpose in their lives are less prone to disease. Purpose is increasingly being touted as the key to navigating the complex, volatile, ambiguous world we face today, where strategy is ever changing and few decisions are obviously right or wrong.

Despite this growing understanding, however, a big challenge remains. In our work training thousands of managers at organizations from GE to the Girl Scouts, and teaching an equal number of executives and students at Harvard Business School, we've found that fewer than 20% of leaders have a strong sense of their own individual purpose. Even fewer can distill their purpose into a concrete statement. They may be able to clearly articulate their organization's mission: Think of Google's "To organize the world's information and make it universally accessible and useful," or Charles Schwab's "A relentless ally for the individual investor." But when asked to describe their own purpose, they typically fall back on something generic and nebulous: "Help others excel." "Ensure success." "Empower my people." Just as problematic, hardly any of them have a clear plan for translating purpose into action. As a result, they limit their aspirations and often fail to achieve their most ambitious professional and personal goals.

Our purpose is to change that—to help executives find and define their leadership purpose and put it to use. Building on the seminal work of our colleague Bill George, our programs initially covered a wide range of topics related to authentic leadership, but in recent years purpose has emerged as the cornerstone of our teaching and coaching. Executives tell us it is the key to accelerating their growth and deepening their impact, in both their professional and personal lives. Indeed, we believe that the process of articulating your purpose and finding the courage to live it—what we call *purpose to impact*—is the single most important developmental task you can undertake as a leader.

Consider Dolf van den Brink, the president and CEO of Heineken USA. Working with us, he identified a decidedly unique purpose statement—"To be the wuxia master who saves the kingdom"—which reflects his love of Chinese kung fu movies, the inspiration he takes from the wise, skillful warriors in them, and the realization that he, too, revels in high-risk situations that compel him to take action. With that impetus, he was able to create a plan for reviving a challenged legacy business during extremely difficult economic conditions. We've also watched a retail operations chief call on his newly clarified purpose—"Compelled to make things better, whomever, wherever, however"—to make the "hard, cage-rattling changes" needed to beat back a global competitor. And we've seen a factory director in Egypt use his purpose—"Create families that excel"—to persuade employees that they should honor the 2012 protest movement not by joining the marches but by maintaining their loyalties to one another and keeping their shared operation running.

We've seen similar results outside the corporate world. Kathi Snook (Scott's wife) is a retired army colonel who'd been struggling to reengage in work after several years as a stay-at-home mom. But

Idea in Brief

The Problem

Purpose is increasingly seen as the key to navigating the complex world we face today, where strategy is ever changing and few decisions are obviously right or wrong. At the same time, few leaders have a strong sense of their own leadership purpose or a clear plan for translating it into action. As a result, they often fail to achieve their most ambitious professional and personal goals.

The Solution

The first step toward uncovering your leadership purpose is to mine your life story for major themes that reveal your lifelong passions and values. Next, craft a concise purpose statement that leaves you emboldened and energized. Finally, develop a *purpose-to-impact plan*. Effective plans:

- Use language that is uniquely meaningful to you

- Focus on big-picture aspirations and then set shorter-term goals, working backward with increasing specificity

- Emphasize the strengths you bring to the table

- Take a holistic view of work and family

after nailing her purpose statement—"To be the gentle, behind-the-scenes, kick-in-the-ass reason for success," something she'd done throughout her military career and with her kids—she decided to run for a hotly contested school committee seat, and won.

And we've implemented this thinking across organizations. Unilever is a company that is committed to purpose-driven leadership, and Jonathan Donner, the head of global learning there, has been a key partner in refining our approach. Working with his company and several other organizations, we've helped more than 1,000 leaders through the purpose-to-impact process and have begun to track and review their progress over the past two to three years. Many have seen dramatic results, ranging from two-step promotions to sustained improvement in business results. Most important, the vast majority tell us they've developed a new ability to thrive in even the most challenging times.

In this article, we share our step-by-step framework to start you down the same path. We'll explain how to identify your purpose and then develop an impact plan to achieve concrete results.

What Is Purpose?

Most of us go to our graves with our music still inside us, unplayed.
—Oliver Wendell Holmes

Your leadership purpose is who you are and what makes you distinctive. Whether you're an entrepreneur at a startup or the CEO of a *Fortune* 500 company, a call center rep or a software developer, your purpose is your brand, what you're driven to achieve, the magic that makes you tick. It's not *what* you do, it's *how* you do your job and *why*—the strengths and passions you bring to the table no matter where you're seated. Although you may express your purpose in different ways in different contexts, it's what everyone close to you recognizes as uniquely you and would miss most if you were gone.

When Kathi shared her purpose statement with her family and friends, the response was instantaneous and overwhelming: "Yes! That's you—all business, all the time!" In every role and every context—as captain of the army gymnastics team, as a math teacher at West Point, informally with her family and friends—she had always led from behind, a gentle but forceful catalyst for others' success. Through this new lens, she was able to see herself—and her future—more clearly. When Dolf van den Brink revealed his newly articulated purpose to his wife, she easily recognized the "wuxia master" who had led his employees through the turmoil of serious fighting and unrest in the Congo and was now ready to attack the challenges at Heineken USA head-on.

At its core, your leadership purpose springs from your identity, the essence of who you are. Purpose is not a list of the education, experience, and skills you've gathered in your life. We'll use ourselves as examples: The fact that Scott is a retired army colonel with an MBA and a PhD is not his purpose. His purpose is "to help others live more 'meaning-full' lives." Purpose is also not a professional title, limited to your current job or organization. Nick's purpose is not "To lead the Authentic Leadership Institute." That's his job. His purpose is "To wake you up and have you find that you are home." He has been doing just that since he was a teenager, and if you sit next to him on the shuttle from Boston to New York, he'll wake you up (figuratively), too. He simply can't help himself.

Purpose is definitely not some jargon-filled catch-all ("Empower my team to achieve exceptional business results while delighting our customers"). It should be specific and personal, resonating with you and you alone. It doesn't have to be aspirational or cause-based ("Save the whales" or "Feed the hungry"). And it's not what you think it should be. It's who you can't help being. In fact, it might not necessarily be all that flattering ("Be the thorn in people's side that keeps them moving!").

How Do You Find It?

To be nobody but yourself in a world which is doing its best, night and day, to make you everybody else, means to fight the hardest battle which any human being can fight; and never stop fighting.

—E.E. Cummings

Finding your leadership purpose is not easy. If it were, we'd all know exactly why we're here and be living that purpose every minute of every day. As E.E. Cummings suggests, we are constantly bombarded by powerful messages (from parents, bosses, management gurus, advertisers, celebrities) about what we should be (smarter, stronger, richer) and about how to lead (empower others, lead from behind, be authentic, distribute power). To figure out who you are in such a world, let alone "be nobody but yourself," is indeed hard work. However, our experience shows that when you have a clear sense of who you are, everything else follows naturally.

Some people will come to the purpose-to-impact journey with a natural bent toward introspection and reflection. Others will find the experience uncomfortable and anxiety-provoking. A few will just roll their eyes. We've worked with leaders of all stripes and can attest that even the most skeptical discover personal and professional value in the experience. At one multinational corporation, we worked with a senior lawyer who characterized himself as "the least likely person to ever find this stuff useful." Yet he became such a supporter that he required all his people to do the program. "I have never read a self-help book, and I don't plan to," he told his staff. "But if you want to become an exceptional leader, you have to know your leadership purpose." The key to engaging both the dreamers and the skeptics is to build a process that has room to express individuality but also offers step-by-step practical guidance.

The first task is to mine your life story for common threads and major themes. The point is to identify your core, lifelong strengths, values, and passions—those pursuits that energize you and bring you joy. We use a variety of prompts but have found three to be most effective:

- What did you especially love doing when you were a child, before the world told you what you should or shouldn't like or do? Describe a moment and how it made you feel.

- Tell us about two of your most challenging life experiences. How have they shaped you?

- What do you enjoy doing in your life now that helps you sing your song?

We strongly recommend grappling with these questions in a small group of a few peers, because we've found that it's almost impossible for people to identify their leadership purpose by themselves. You can't get a clear picture of yourself without trusted colleagues or friends to act as mirrors.

After this reflective work, take a shot at crafting a clear, concise, and declarative statement of purpose: "My leadership purpose is ____." The words in your purpose statement must be yours. They must capture your essence. And they must call you to action.

To give you an idea of how the process works, consider the experiences of a few executives. When we asked one manager about her childhood passions, she told us about growing up in rural Scotland and delighting in "discovery" missions. One day, she and a friend set out determined to find frogs and spent the whole day going from pond to pond, turning over every stone. Just before dark, she discovered a single frog and was triumphant. The purpose statement she later crafted—"Always find the frogs!"—is perfect for her current role as the senior VP of R&D for her company.

Another executive used two "crucible" life experiences to craft her purpose. The first was personal: Years before, as a divorced young mother of two, she found herself homeless and begging on the street, but she used her wits to get back on her feet. The second was professional: During the economic crisis of 2008, she had to oversee her company's retrenchment from Asia and was tasked with closing the flagship operation in the region. Despite the near hopeless job environment, she was able to help every one of her employees find another job before letting them go. After discussing these stories with her group, she shifted her purpose statement from "Continually and consistently develop and facilitate the growth and development of myself and others leading to great performance" to "With tenacity, create brilliance."

Dolf came to his "wuxia master" statement after exploring not only his film preferences but also his extraordinary crucible experience in the Congo, when militants were threatening the brewery he managed and he had to order it barricaded to protect his employees and prevent looting. The Egyptian factory director focused on family as his purpose because his stories revealed that familial love and

Purpose statements

From bad ...	To good
Lead new markets department to achieve exceptional business results	Eliminate "chaos"
Be a driver in the infrastructure business that allows each person to achieve their needed outcomes while also mastering the new drivers of our business as I balance my family and work demands	Bring water and power to the 2 billion people who do not have it
Continually and consistently develop and facilitate the growth and development of myself and others, leading to great performance	With tenacity, create brilliance

support had been the key to facing every challenge in his life, while the retail operations chief used "Compelled to improve" after realizing that his greatest achievements had always come when he pushed himself and others out of their comfort zones.

As you review your stories, you will see a unifying thread, just as these executives did. Pull it, and you'll uncover your purpose. (The exhibit "Purpose statements: from bad to good" offers a sampling of purpose statements.)

How Do You Put Your Purpose into Action?

This is the true joy in life, the being used for a purpose recognized by yourself as a mighty one.

—George Bernard Shaw

Clarifying your purpose as a leader is critical, but writing the statement is not enough. You must also envision the impact you'll have on your world as a result of living your purpose. Your actions—not your words—are what really matter. Of course, it's virtually impossible for any of us to fully live into our purpose 100% of the time. But with work and careful planning, we can do it more often, more consciously, wholeheartedly, and effectively.

Purpose-to-impact plans differ from traditional development plans in several important ways: They start with a statement of leadership purpose rather than of a business or career goal. They take a holistic view of professional and personal life rather than ignore the fact that you have a family or outside interests and commitments. They incorporate meaningful, purpose-infused language to create a document that speaks to you, not just to any person in your job or role. They force you to envision long-term opportunities for living your purpose (three to five years out) and then help you to work backward from there (two years out, one year, six months, three months, 30 days) to set specific goals for achieving them.

When executives approach development in this purpose-driven way, their aspirations—for instance, Kathi's decision to get involved in the school board, or the Egyptian factory director's ambition to

Purpose-to-impact planning	Traditional development planning
Uses meaningful, purpose-infused language	Uses standard business language
Is focused on strengths to realize career aspirations	Is focused on weaknesses to address performance
Elicits a statement of leadership purpose that explains how you will lead	States a business- or career-driven goal
Sets incremental goals related to living your leadership purpose	Measures success using metrics tied to the firm's mission and goals
Focuses on the future, working backward	Focuses on the present, working forward
Is unique to you; addresses who you are as a leader	Is generic; addresses the job or role
Takes a holistic view of work and family	Ignores goals and responsibilities outside the office

run manufacturing and logistics across the Middle East—are stoked. Leaders also become more energized in their current roles. Dolf's impact plan inspired him to tackle his role at Heineken USA with four mottos for his team: "Be brave," "Decide and do," "Hunt as a pack," and "Take it personally." When Unilever executive Jostein Solheim created a development plan around his purpose—"To be part of a global movement that makes changing the world seem fun and achievable"—he realized he wanted to stay on as CEO of the Ben & Jerry's business rather than moving up the corporate ladder.

Let's now look at a hypothetical purpose-to-impact plan (representing a composite of several people with whom we've worked) for an in-depth view of the process. "Richard" arrived at his purpose only after being prodded into talking about his lifelong passion for sailing; suddenly, he'd found a set of experiences and language that could redefine how he saw his job in procurement.

Richard's development plan leads with the **purpose statement** he crafted: "To harness all the elements to win the race." This is followed by **an explanation** of why that's his purpose: Research shows

A Purpose-to-Impact Plan

THIS SAMPLE PLAN shows how "Richard" uses his unique leadership purpose to envision big-picture aspirations and then work backward to set more-specific goals.

1. Create purpose statement

To harness all the elements to win the race

2. Write explanation

I love to sail. In my teens and 20s, I raced high-performance three-man skiffs and almost made it to the Olympics. Now sailing is my hobby and passion— a challenge that requires discipline, balance, and coordination. You never know what the wind will do next, and in the end, you win the race only by relying on your team's combined capabilities, intuition, and flow. It's all about how you read the elements.

3. Set three- to five-year goals

Be known for training the best crews and winning the big races: Take on a global procurement role and use the opportunity to push my organization ahead of competitors

How will I do it?

- Make everyone feel they're part of the same team
- Navigate unpredictable conditions by seeing wind shears before everyone else
- Keep calm when we lose individual races; learn and prepare for the next ones

Celebrate my shore team: Make sure the family has one thing we do that binds us

4. Set two-year goals

Win the gold: Implement a new procurement model, redefining our relationship with suppliers and generating 10% cost savings for the company

Tackle next-level racing challenge: Move into a European role with broader responsibilities

How will I do it?

- Anticipate and then face the tough challenges
- Insist on innovative yet rigorous and pragmatic solutions
- Assemble and train the winning crew

Develop my shore team: Teach the boys to sail

5. Set one-year goals
Target the gold: Begin to develop new procurement process

Win the short race: Deliver Sympix project ahead of expectations

Build a seaworthy boat: Keep TFLS process within cost and cash forecast

How will I do it?

- Accelerate team reconfiguration
- Get buy-in from management for new procurement approach

  Invest in my shore team: Take a two-week vacation, no email

6. Map out critical next steps
Assemble the crew: Finalize key hires

Chart the course: Lay the groundwork for Sympix and TFLS projects

How will I do it?
Six months:

- Finalize succession plans
- Set out Sympix timeline

Three months:

- Land a world-class replacement for Jim
- Schedule "action windows" to focus with no email

30 days:

- Bring Alex in Shanghai on board
- Agree on TFLS metrics
- Conduct one-day Sympix offsite

Reconnect with my shore team: Be more present with Jill and the boys

7. Examine key relationships
Sarah, HR manager

Jill, manager of my "shore team"

that understanding what motivates us dramatically increases our ability to achieve big goals.

Next, Richard addresses his **three- to five-year goals** using the language of his purpose statement. We find that this is a good time frame to target first; several years is long enough that even the most disillusioned managers could imagine they'd actually be living into their purpose by then. But it's not so distant that it creates complacency. A goal might be to land a top job—in Richard's case, a global procurement role—but the focus should be on how you will do it, what kind of leader you'll be.

Then he considers **two-year goals**. This is a time frame in which the grand future and current reality begin to merge. What new responsibilities will you take on? What do you have to do to set yourself up for the longer term? Remember to address your personal life, too, because you should be more fully living into your purpose everywhere. Richard's goals explicitly reference his family, or "shore team."

The fifth step—setting **one-year goals**—is often the most challenging. Many people ask, "What if most of what I am doing today isn't aligned in any way with my leadership purpose? How do I get from here to there?" We've found two ways to address this problem. First, think about whether you can rewrite the narrative on parts of your work, or change the way you do some tasks, so that they become an expression of your purpose. For example, the phrase "seaworthy boat" helps Richard see the meaning in managing a basic procurement process. Second, consider whether you can add an activity that is 100% aligned with your purpose. We've found that most people can manage to devote 5% to 10% of their time to something that energizes them and helps others see their strengths. Take Richard's decision to contribute to the global strategic procurement effort: It's not part of his "day job," but it gets him involved in a more purpose-driven project.

Now we get to the nitty-gritty. What are the **critical next steps** that you must take in the coming six months, three months, and 30 days to accomplish the one-year goals you've set out? The importance of small wins is well documented in almost every management discipline from change initiatives to innovation. In detailing your next steps, don't write down all the requirements of your job. List the activities or results that are most critical given your newly clarified leadership purpose and ambitions. You'll probably notice that a number of your tasks seem much less urgent than they did before, while others you had pushed to the side take priority.

Finally, we look at the **key relationships** needed to turn your plan into reality. Identify two or three people who can help you live more fully into your leadership purpose. For Richard, it is Sarah, the HR manager who will help him assemble his crew, and his wife, Jill, the manager of his "shore team."

Executives tell us that their individual purpose-to-impact plans help them stay true to their short- and long-term goals, inspiring courage, commitment, and focus. When they're frustrated or flagging, they pull out the plans to remind themselves what they want to accomplish and how they'll succeed. After creating his plan, the retail operations chief facing global competition said he's no longer "shying away from things that are too hard." Dolf van den Brink said: "I'm much clearer on where I really can contribute and where not. I have full clarity on the kind of roles I aspire to and can make explicit choices along the way."

What creates the greatest leaders and companies? Each of them operates from a slightly different set of assumptions about the world, their industry, what can or can't be done. That individual perspective allows them to create great value and have significant impact. They all operate with a unique leadership purpose. To be a truly effective leader, you must do the same. Clarify your purpose, and put it to work.

Originally published in May 2014. Reprint R1405H

Creating Shared Value

by Michael E. Porter and Mark R. Kramer

THE CAPITALIST SYSTEM is under siege. In recent years business increasingly has been viewed as a major cause of social, environmental, and economic problems. Companies are widely perceived to be prospering at the expense of the broader community.

Even worse, the more business has begun to embrace corporate responsibility, the more it has been blamed for society's failures. The legitimacy of business has fallen to levels not seen in recent history. This diminished trust in business leads political leaders to set policies that undermine competitiveness and sap economic growth. Business is caught in a vicious circle.

A big part of the problem lies with companies themselves, which remain trapped in an outdated approach to value creation that has emerged over the past few decades. They continue to view value creation narrowly, optimizing short-term financial performance in a bubble while missing the most important customer needs and ignoring the broader influences that determine their longer-term success. How else could companies overlook the well-being of their customers, the depletion of natural resources vital to their businesses, the viability of key suppliers, or the economic distress of the communities in which they produce and sell? How else could companies think that simply shifting activities to locations with ever lower wages was a sustainable "solution" to competitive challenges? Government and civil society have often exacerbated the problem by attempting to address social weaknesses at the expense of business. The presumed trade-offs between economic efficiency and social progress have been institutionalized in decades of policy choices.

Companies must take the lead in bringing business and society back together. The recognition is there among sophisticated business and thought leaders, and promising elements of a new model are emerging. Yet we still lack an overall framework for guiding these efforts, and most companies remain stuck in a "social responsibility" mindset in which societal issues are at the periphery, not the core.

The solution lies in the principle of shared value, which involves creating economic value in a way that *also* creates value for society by addressing its needs and challenges. Businesses must reconnect company success with social progress. Shared value is not social responsibility, philanthropy, or even sustainability, but a new way to achieve economic success. It is not on the margin of what companies do but at the center. We believe that it can give rise to the next major transformation of business thinking.

A growing number of companies known for their hard-nosed approach to business—such as GE, Google, IBM, Intel, Johnson & Johnson, Nestlé, Unilever, and Walmart—have already embarked on important efforts to create shared value by reconceiving the intersection between society and corporate performance. Yet our recognition of the transformative power of shared value is still in its genesis. Realizing it will require leaders and managers to develop new skills and knowledge—such as a far deeper appreciation of societal needs, a greater understanding of the true bases of company productivity, and the ability to collaborate across profit/nonprofit boundaries. And government must learn how to regulate in ways that enable shared value rather than work against it.

Capitalism is an unparalleled vehicle for meeting human needs, improving efficiency, creating jobs, and building wealth. But a narrow conception of capitalism has prevented business from harnessing its full potential to meet society's broader challenges. The opportunities have been there all along but have been overlooked. Businesses acting as businesses, not as charitable donors, are the

Idea in Brief

The concept of shared value—which focuses on the connections between societal and economic progress—has the power to unleash the next wave of global growth.

An increasing number of companies known for their hard-nosed approach to business—such as Google, IBM, Intel, Johnson & Johnson, Nestlé, Unilever, and Walmart—have begun to embark on important shared value initiatives. But our understanding of the potential of shared value is just beginning.

There are three key ways that companies can create shared value opportunities:

- By reconceiving products and markets

- By redefining productivity in the value chain

- By enabling local cluster development

Every firm should look at decisions and opportunities through the lens of shared value. This will lead to new approaches that generate greater innovation and growth for companies—and also greater benefits for society.

most powerful force for addressing the pressing issues we face. The moment for a new conception of capitalism is now; society's needs are large and growing, while customers, employees, and a new generation of young people are asking business to step up.

The purpose of the corporation must be redefined as creating shared value, not just profit per se. This will drive the next wave of innovation and productivity growth in the global economy. It will also reshape capitalism and its relationship to society. Perhaps most important of all, learning how to create shared value is our best chance to legitimize business again.

Moving Beyond Trade-Offs

Business and society have been pitted against each other for too long. That is in part because economists have legitimized the idea that to provide societal benefits, companies must temper their economic success. In neoclassical thinking, a requirement for social improvement—such as safety or hiring the disabled—imposes a constraint on the corporation. Adding a constraint to a firm that is already maximizing profits, says the theory, will inevitably raise costs and reduce those profits.

A related concept, with the same conclusion, is the notion of externalities. Externalities arise when firms create social costs that they do not have to bear, such as pollution. Thus, society must impose taxes, regulations, and penalties so that firms "internalize" these externalities—a belief influencing many government policy decisions.

This perspective has also shaped the strategies of firms themselves, which have largely excluded social and environmental considerations from their economic thinking. Firms have taken the broader context in which they do business as a given and resisted regulatory standards as invariably contrary to their interests. Solving social problems has been ceded to governments and to NGOs. Corporate responsibility programs—a reaction to external pressure—have emerged largely to improve firms' reputations and are treated as a necessary expense. Anything more is seen by many as an irresponsible use of shareholders' money. Governments, for their part, have often regulated in a way that makes shared value more difficult to achieve. Implicitly, each side has assumed that the other is an obstacle to pursuing its goals and acted accordingly.

The concept of shared value, in contrast, recognizes that societal needs, not just conventional economic needs, define markets. It also recognizes that social harms or weaknesses frequently create *internal* costs for firms—such as wasted energy or raw materials, costly accidents, and the need for remedial training to compensate for inadequacies in education. And addressing societal harms and constraints does not necessarily raise costs for firms, because they can innovate through using new technologies, operating methods, and management approaches—and as a result, increase their productivity and expand their markets.

Shared value, then, is not about personal values. Nor is it about "sharing" the value already created by firms—a redistribution approach. Instead, it is about expanding the total pool of economic and social value. A good example of this difference in perspective is the fair trade movement in purchasing. Fair trade aims to increase the proportion of revenue that goes to poor farmers by paying them higher prices for the same crops. Though this may be a noble sentiment, fair trade is mostly about redistribution rather than expanding the overall amount of value created. A shared value perspective, instead, focuses on improving growing techniques and strengthening the local cluster of supporting suppliers and other institutions in order to increase farmers' efficiency, yields, product quality, and sustainability. This leads to a bigger pie of revenue and profits that benefits both farmers and the companies that buy from them. Early studies of cocoa farmers in the Côte d'Ivoire, for instance, suggest that while fair trade can increase farmers' incomes by 10% to 20%, shared value investments can raise their incomes by more than 300%. Initial investment and time may be required to implement new procurement practices and develop the supporting cluster, but the return will be greater economic value and broader strategic benefits for all participants.

The Roots of Shared Value

At a very basic level, the competitiveness of a company and the health of the communities around it are closely intertwined. A business needs a successful community, not only to create demand for its products but also to provide critical public assets and a supportive environment. A community needs successful businesses to provide jobs and wealth creation opportunities for its citizens. This interdependence means that public policies that undermine the productivity and competitiveness of businesses are self-defeating, especially in a global economy where facilities and jobs can easily move elsewhere. NGOs and governments have not always appreciated this connection.

In the old, narrow view of capitalism, business contributes to society by making a profit, which supports employment, wages, purchases, investments, and taxes. Conducting business as usual is sufficient social benefit. A firm is largely a self-contained entity, and

What Is "Shared Value"?

THE CONCEPT OF SHARED VALUE CAN BE DEFINED as policies and operating practices that enhance the competitiveness of a company while simultaneously advancing the economic and social conditions in the communities in which it operates. Shared value creation focuses on identifying and expanding the connections between societal and economic progress.

The concept rests on the premise that both economic and social progress must be addressed using value principles. Value is defined as benefits relative to costs, not just benefits alone. Value creation is an idea that has long been recognized in business, where profit is revenues earned from customers minus the costs incurred. However, businesses have rarely approached societal issues from a value perspective but have treated them as peripheral matters. This has obscured the connections between economic and social concerns.

In the social sector, thinking in value terms is even less common. Social organizations and government entities often see success solely in terms of the benefits achieved or the money expended. As governments and NGOs begin to think more in value terms, their interest in collaborating with business will inevitably grow.

---

social or community issues fall outside its proper scope. (This is the argument advanced persuasively by Milton Friedman in his critique of the whole notion of corporate social responsibility.)

This perspective has permeated management thinking for the past two decades. Firms focused on enticing consumers to buy more and more of their products. Facing growing competition and shorter-term performance pressures from shareholders, managers resorted to waves of restructuring, personnel reductions, and relocation to lower-cost regions, while leveraging balance sheets to return capital to investors. The results were often commoditization, price competition, little true innovation, slow organic growth, and no clear competitive advantage.

In this kind of competition, the communities in which companies operate perceive little benefit even as profits rise. Instead, they perceive that profits come at their expense, an impression that has become even stronger in the current economic recovery, in which rising earnings have done little to offset high unemployment, local business distress, and severe pressures on community services.

It was not always this way. The best companies once took on a broad range of roles in meeting the needs of workers, communities, and supporting businesses. As other social institutions appeared on the scene, however, these roles fell away or were delegated. Shortening investor time horizons began to narrow thinking about appropriate investments. As the vertically integrated firm gave way to greater reliance on outside vendors, outsourcing and offshoring weakened the connection between firms and their communities. As firms moved disparate activities to more and more locations, they often lost touch with any location. Indeed, many companies no longer recognize a home—but see themselves as "global" companies.

These transformations drove major progress in economic efficiency. However, something profoundly important was lost in the process, as more-fundamental opportunities for value creation were missed. The scope of strategic thinking contracted.

Strategy theory holds that to be successful, a company must create a distinctive value proposition that meets the needs of a chosen set of customers. The firm gains competitive advantage from how it configures the value chain, or the set of activities involved in creating, producing, selling, delivering, and supporting its products or services. For decades businesspeople have studied positioning and the best ways to design activities and integrate them. However, companies have overlooked opportunities to meet fundamental societal needs and misunderstood how societal harms and weaknesses affect value chains. Our field of vision has simply been too narrow.

In understanding the business environment, managers have focused most of their attention on the industry, or the particular business in which the firm competes. This is because industry structure has a decisive impact on a firm's profitability. What has been missed, however, is the profound effect that location can have on productivity and innovation. Companies have failed to grasp the importance of the broader business environment surrounding their major operations.

How Shared Value Is Created

Companies can create economic value by creating societal value. There are three distinct ways to do this: by reconceiving products and markets, redefining productivity in the value chain, and building supportive industry clusters at the company's locations. Each of these is part of the virtuous circle of shared value; improving value in one area gives rise to opportunities in the others.

The concept of shared value resets the boundaries of capitalism. By better connecting companies' success with societal improvement, it opens up many ways to serve new needs, gain efficiency, create differentiation, and expand markets.

The ability to create shared value applies equally to advanced economies and developing countries, though the specific opportunities will differ. The opportunities will also differ markedly across industries and companies—but every company has them. And their range and scope is far broader than has been recognized. *[The idea of shared value was initially explored in a December 2006 HBR article by Michael E. Porter and Mark R. Kramer, "Strategy and Society: The Link Between Competitive Advantage and Corporate Social Responsibility."]*

Reconceiving Products and Markets

Society's needs are huge—health, better housing, improved nutrition, help for the aging, greater financial security, less environmental damage. Arguably, they are the greatest unmet needs in the global economy. In business we have spent decades learning how to parse and manufacture demand while missing the most important demand of all. Too many companies have lost sight of that most basic of questions: Is our product good for our customers? Or for our customers' customers?

In advanced economies, demand for products and services that meet societal needs is rapidly growing. Food companies that traditionally concentrated on taste and quantity to drive more and more consumption are refocusing on the fundamental need for better

Blurring the Profit/Nonprofit Boundary

THE CONCEPT OF SHARED VALUE BLURS THE LINE between for-profit and nonprofit organizations. New kinds of hybrid enterprises are rapidly appearing. For example, WaterHealth International, a fast-growing for-profit, uses innovative water purification techniques to distribute clean water at minimal cost to more than one million people in rural India, Ghana, and the Philippines. Its investors include not only the socially focused Acumen Fund and the International Finance Corporation of the World Bank but also Dow Chemical's venture fund. Revolution Foods, a four-year-old venture-capital-backed U.S. startup, provides 60,000 fresh, healthful, and nutritious meals to students daily—and does so at a higher gross margin than traditional competitors. Waste Concern, a hybrid profit/nonprofit enterprise started in Bangladesh 15 years ago, has built the capacity to convert 700 tons of trash, collected daily from neighborhood slums, into organic fertilizer, thereby increasing crop yields and reducing CO_2 emissions. Seeded with capital from the Lions Club and the United Nations Development Programme, the company improves health conditions while earning a substantial gross margin through fertilizer sales and carbon credits.

The blurring of the boundary between successful for-profits and nonprofits is one of the strong signs that creating shared value is possible.

---

nutrition. Intel and IBM are both devising ways to help utilities harness digital intelligence in order to economize on power usage. Wells Fargo has developed a line of products and tools that help customers budget, manage credit, and pay down debt. Sales of GE's Ecomagination products reached $18 billion in 2009—the size of a *Fortune* 150 company. GE now predicts that revenues of Ecomagination products will grow at twice the rate of total company revenues over the next five years.

In these and many other ways, whole new avenues for innovation open up, and shared value is created. Society's gains are even greater, because businesses will often be far more effective than governments and nonprofits are at marketing that motivates customers to embrace products and services that create societal benefits, like healthier food or environmentally friendly products.

Equal or greater opportunities arise from serving disadvantaged communities and developing countries. Though societal needs are even more pressing there, these communities have not been recognized as viable markets. Today attention is riveted on India, China, and increasingly, Brazil, which offer firms the prospect of reaching billions of new customers at the bottom of the pyramid—a notion persuasively articulated by C.K. Prahalad. Yet these countries have always had huge needs, as do many developing countries.

Similar opportunities await in nontraditional communities in advanced countries. We have learned, for example, that poor urban areas are America's most underserved market; their substantial concentrated purchasing power has often been overlooked. (See the research of the Initiative for a Competitive Inner City, at icic.org.)

The societal benefits of providing appropriate products to lower-income and disadvantaged consumers can be profound, while the profits for companies can be substantial. For example, low-priced cell phones that provide mobile banking services are helping the poor save money securely and transforming the ability of small farmers to produce and market their crops. In Kenya, Vodafone's M-PESA mobile banking service signed up 10 million customers in three years; the funds it handles now represent 11% of that country's GDP. In India, Thomson Reuters has developed a promising monthly service for farmers who earn an average of $2,000 a year. For a fee of $5 a quarter, it provides weather and crop-pricing information and agricultural advice. The service reaches an estimated 2 million farmers, and early research indicates that it has helped increase the incomes of more than 60% of them—in some cases even tripling incomes. As capitalism begins to work in poorer communities, new opportunities for economic development and social progress increase exponentially.

For a company, the starting point for creating this kind of shared value is to identify all the societal needs, benefits, and harms that are or could be embodied in the firm's products. The opportunities are not static; they change constantly as technology evolves, economies develop, and societal priorities shift. An ongoing exploration of societal needs will lead companies to discover new opportunities for differentiation and repositioning in traditional markets, and to recognize the potential of new markets they previously overlooked.

The connection between competitive advantage and social issues

There are numerous ways in which addressing societal concerns can yield productivity benefits to a firm. Consider, for example, what happens when a firm invests in a wellness program. Society benefits because employees and their families become healthier, and the firm minimizes employee absences and lost productivity. The graphic below depicts some areas where the connections are strongest.

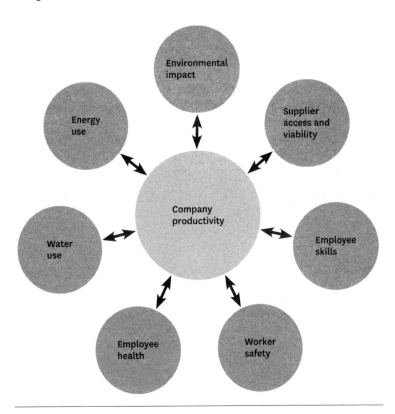

Meeting needs in underserved markets often requires redesigned products or different distribution methods. These requirements can trigger fundamental innovations that also have application in traditional markets. Microfinance, for example, was invented to serve unmet financing needs in developing countries. Now it is growing rapidly in the United States, where it is filling an important gap that was unrecognized.

Redefining Productivity in the Value Chain

A company's value chain inevitably affects—and is affected by—numerous societal issues, such as natural resource and water use, health and safety, working conditions, and equal treatment in the workplace. Opportunities to create shared value arise because societal problems can create economic costs in the firm's value chain. Many so-called externalities actually inflict internal costs on the firm, even in the absence of regulation or resource taxes. Excess packaging of products and greenhouse gases are not just costly to the environment but costly to the business. Walmart, for example, was able to address both issues by reducing its packaging and rerouting its trucks to cut 100 million miles from its delivery routes in 2009, saving $200 million even as it shipped more products. Innovation in disposing of plastic used in stores has saved millions in lower disposal costs to landfills.

The new thinking reveals that the congruence between societal progress and productivity in the value chain is far greater than traditionally believed (see the exhibit "The connection between competitive advantage and social issues"). The synergy increases when firms approach societal issues from a shared value perspective and invent new ways of operating to address them. So far, however, few companies have reaped the full productivity benefits in areas such as health, safety, environmental performance, and employee retention and capability.

But there are unmistakable signs of change. Efforts to minimize pollution were once thought to inevitably increase business costs—and to occur only because of regulation and taxes. Today there is a growing consensus that major improvements in environmental performance can often be achieved with better technology at nominal incremental cost and can even yield net cost savings through enhanced resource utilization, process efficiency, and quality.

In each of the areas in the exhibit, a deeper understanding of productivity and a growing awareness of the fallacy of short-term cost reductions (which often actually lower productivity or make it unsustainable) are giving rise to new approaches. The following are some of the most important ways in which shared value thinking is transforming the value chain, which are not independent but often mutually reinforcing. Efforts in these and other areas are still works in process, whose implications will be felt for years to come.

Energy use and logistics

The use of energy throughout the value chain is being reexamined, whether it be in processes, transportation, buildings, supply chains, distribution channels, or support services. Triggered by energy price spikes and a new awareness of opportunities for energy efficiency, this reexamination was under way even before carbon emissions became a global focus. The result has been striking improvements in energy utilization through better technology, recycling, cogeneration, and numerous other practices—all of which create shared value.

We are learning that shipping is expensive, not just because of energy costs and emissions but because it adds time, complexity, inventory costs, and management costs. Logistical systems are beginning to be redesigned to reduce shipping distances, streamline handling, improve vehicle routing, and the like. All of these steps create shared value. The British retailer Marks & Spencer's ambitious overhaul of its supply chain, for example, which involves steps as simple as stopping the purchase of supplies from one hemisphere to ship to another, is expected to save the retailer £175 million annually by fiscal 2016, while hugely reducing carbon emissions. In the process of reexamining logistics, thinking about outsourcing and location will also be revised (as we will discuss below).

Resource use

Heightened environmental awareness and advances in technology are catalyzing new approaches in areas such as utilization of water, raw materials, and packaging, as well as expanding recycling and reuse. The opportunities apply to all resources, not just those that have been identified by environmentalists. Better resource utilization—enabled by improving technology—will permeate all parts of the value chain and will spread to suppliers and channels. Landfills will fill more slowly.

For example, Coca-Cola has already reduced its worldwide water consumption by 9% from a 2004 baseline—nearly halfway to its goal of a 20% reduction by 2012. Dow Chemical managed to reduce consumption of fresh water at its largest production site by one billion gallons—enough water to supply nearly 40,000 people in the United States for a year—resulting in savings of $4 million. The demand for water-saving technology has allowed India's Jain Irrigation, a leading global manufacturer of complete drip irrigation systems for water conservation, to achieve a 41% compound annual growth rate in revenue over the past five years.

Procurement

The traditional playbook calls for companies to commoditize and exert maximum bargaining power on suppliers to drive down prices—even when purchasing from small businesses or subsistence-level farmers. More recently, firms have been rapidly outsourcing to suppliers in lower-wage locations.

Today some companies are beginning to understand that marginalized suppliers cannot remain productive or sustain, much less improve, their quality. By increasing access to inputs, sharing technology, and providing financing, companies can improve supplier quality and productivity while ensuring access to growing volume. Improving productivity will often trump lower prices. As suppliers get stronger, their environmental impact often falls dramatically, which further improves their efficiency. Shared value is created.

The Role of Social Entrepreneurs

BUSINESSES ARE NOT THE ONLY PLAYERS in finding profitable solutions to social problems. A whole generation of social entrepreneurs is pioneering new product concepts that meet social needs using viable business models. Because they are not locked into narrow traditional business thinking, social entrepreneurs are often well ahead of established corporations in discovering these opportunities. Social enterprises that create shared value can scale up far more rapidly than purely social programs, which often suffer from an inability to grow and become self-sustaining.

Real social entrepreneurship should be measured by its ability to create shared value, not just social benefit.

A good example of such new procurement thinking can be found at Nespresso, one of Nestlé's fastest-growing divisions, which has enjoyed annual growth of 30% since 2000. Nespresso combines a sophisticated espresso machine with single-cup aluminum capsules containing ground coffees from around the world. Offering quality and convenience, Nespresso has expanded the market for premium coffee.

Obtaining a reliable supply of specialized coffees is extremely challenging, however. Most coffees are grown by small farmers in impoverished rural areas of Africa and Latin America, who are trapped in a cycle of low productivity, poor quality, and environmental degradation that limits production volume. To address these issues, Nestlé redesigned procurement. It worked intensively with its growers, providing advice on farming practices, guaranteeing bank loans, and helping secure inputs such as plant stock, pesticides, and fertilizers. Nestlé established local facilities to measure the quality of the coffee at the point of purchase, which allowed it to pay a premium for better beans directly to the growers and thus improve their incentives. Greater yield per hectare and higher production quality increased growers' incomes, and the environmental impact of farms shrank. Meanwhile, Nestlé's reliable supply of good coffee grew significantly. Shared value was created.

Embedded in the Nestlé example is a far broader insight, which is the advantage of buying from capable local suppliers. Outsourcing to other locations and countries creates transaction costs and inefficiencies that can offset lower wage and input costs. Capable local suppliers help firms avoid these costs and can reduce cycle time, increase flexibility, foster faster learning, and enable innovation. Buying local includes not only local companies but also local units of national or international companies. When firms buy locally, their suppliers can get stronger, increase their profits, hire more people, and pay better wages—all of which will benefit other businesses in the community. Shared value is created.

Distribution

Companies are beginning to reexamine distribution practices from a shared value perspective. As iTunes, Kindle, and Google Scholar (which offers texts of scholarly literature online) demonstrate, profitable new distribution models can also dramatically reduce paper and plastic usage. Similarly, microfinance has created a cost-efficient new model of distributing financial services to small businesses.

Opportunities for new distribution models can be even greater in nontraditional markets. For example, Hindustan Unilever is creating a new direct-to-home distribution system, run by underprivileged female entrepreneurs, in Indian villages of fewer than 2,000 people. Unilever provides microcredit and training and now has more than 45,000 entrepreneurs covering some 100,000 villages across 15 Indian states. Project Shakti, as this distribution system is called, benefits communities not only by giving women skills that often double their household income but also by reducing the spread of communicable diseases through increased access to hygiene products. This is a good example of how the unique ability of business to market to hard-to-reach consumers can benefit society by getting life-altering products into the hands of people that need them. Project Shakti now accounts for 5% of Unilever's total revenues in India and has extended the company's reach into rural areas and built its brand in media-dark regions, creating major economic value for the company.

Employee productivity

The focus on holding down wage levels, reducing benefits, and offshoring is beginning to give way to an awareness of the positive effects that a living wage, safety, wellness, training, and opportunities for advancement for employees have on productivity. Many companies, for example, traditionally sought to minimize the cost of "expensive" employee health-care coverage or even eliminate health coverage altogether. Today leading companies have learned that because of lost workdays and diminished employee productivity, poor health costs them more than health benefits do. Take Johnson & Johnson. By helping employees stop smoking (a two-thirds reduction in the past 15 years) and implementing numerous other wellness programs, the company has saved $250 million on health-care costs, a return of $2.71 for every dollar spent on wellness from 2002 to 2008. Moreover, Johnson & Johnson has benefited from a more present and productive workforce. If labor unions focused more on shared value, too, these kinds of employee approaches would spread even faster.

Location

Business thinking has embraced the myth that location no longer matters, because logistics are inexpensive, information flows rapidly, and markets are global. The cheaper the location, then, the better. Concern about the local communities in which a company operates has faded.

That oversimplified thinking is now being challenged, partly by the rising costs of energy and carbon emissions but also by a greater recognition of the productivity cost of highly dispersed production systems and the hidden costs of distant procurement discussed earlier. Walmart, for example, is increasingly sourcing produce for its food sections from local farms near its warehouses. It has discovered that the savings on transportation costs and the ability to restock in smaller quantities more than offset the lower prices of industrial farms farther away. Nestlé is establishing smaller plants closer to its markets and stepping up efforts to maximize the use of locally available materials.

The calculus of locating activities in developing countries is also changing. Olam International, a leading cashew producer, traditionally shipped its nuts from Africa to Asia for processing at facilities staffed by productive Asian workers. But by opening local processing plants and training workers in Tanzania, Mozambique, Nigeria, and Côte d'Ivoire, Olam has cut processing and shipping costs by as much as 25%—not to mention, greatly reduced carbon emissions. In making this move, Olam also built preferred relationships with local farmers. And it has provided direct employment to 17,000 people—95% of whom are women—and indirect employment to an equal number of people, in rural areas where jobs otherwise were not available.

These trends may well lead companies to remake their value chains by moving some activities closer to home and having fewer major production locations. Until now, many companies have thought that being global meant moving production to locations with the lowest labor costs and designing their supply chains to achieve the most immediate impact on expenses. In reality, the strongest international competitors will often be those that can establish deeper roots in important communities. Companies that can embrace this new locational thinking will create shared value.

As these examples illustrate, reimagining value chains from the perspective of shared value will offer significant new ways to innovate and unlock new economic value that most businesses have missed.

Enabling Local Cluster Development

No company is self-contained. The success of every company is affected by the supporting companies and infrastructure around it. Productivity and innovation are strongly influenced by "clusters," or geographic concentrations of firms, related businesses, suppliers, service providers, and logistical infrastructure in a particular field—such as IT in Silicon Valley, cut flowers in Kenya, and diamond cutting in Surat, India.

Clusters include not only businesses but institutions such as academic programs, trade associations, and standards organizations. They also draw on the broader public assets in the surrounding community, such as schools and universities, clean water, fair-competition laws, quality standards, and market transparency.

Clusters are prominent in all successful and growing regional economies and play a crucial role in driving productivity, innovation, and competitiveness. Capable local suppliers foster greater logistical efficiency and ease of collaboration, as we have discussed. Stronger local capabilities in such areas as training, transportation services, and related industries also boost productivity. Without a supporting cluster, conversely, productivity suffers.

Deficiencies in the framework conditions surrounding the cluster also create internal costs for firms. Poor public education imposes productivity and remedial-training costs. Poor transportation infrastructure drives up the costs of logistics. Gender or racial discrimination reduces the pool of capable employees. Poverty limits the demand for products and leads to environmental degradation, unhealthy workers, and high security costs. As companies have increasingly become disconnected from their communities, however, their influence in solving these problems has waned even as their costs have grown.

Firms create shared value by building clusters to improve company productivity while addressing gaps or failures in the framework conditions surrounding the cluster. Efforts to develop or attract capable suppliers, for example, enable the procurement benefits we discussed earlier. A focus on clusters and location has been all but absent in management thinking. Cluster thinking has also been missing in many economic development initiatives, which have failed because they involved isolated interventions and overlooked critical complementary investments.

A key aspect of cluster building in developing and developed countries alike is the formation of open and transparent markets. In inefficient or monopolized markets where workers are exploited, where suppliers do not receive fair prices, and where price transparency is lacking, productivity suffers. Enabling fair and open markets,

Creating Shared Value: Implications for Government and Civil Society

WHILE OUR FOCUS HERE IS PRIMARILY ON COMPANIES, the principles of shared value apply equally to governments and nonprofit organizations.

Governments and NGOs will be most effective if they think in value terms—considering benefits relative to costs—and focus on the results achieved rather than the funds and effort expended. Activists have tended to approach social improvement from an ideological or absolutist perspective, as if social benefits should be pursued at any cost. Governments and NGOs often assume that trade-offs between economic and social benefits are inevitable, exacerbating these trade-offs through their approaches. For example, much environmental regulation still takes the form of command-and-control mandates and enforcement actions designed to embarrass and punish companies.

Regulators would accomplish much more by focusing on measuring environmental performance and introducing standards, phase-in periods, and support for technology that would promote innovation, improve the environment, and increase competitiveness simultaneously.

The principle of shared value creation cuts across the traditional divide between the responsibilities of business and those of government or civil society. From society's perspective, it does not matter what types of organizations created the value. What matters is that benefits are delivered by those organizations—or combinations of organizations—that are best positioned to achieve the most impact for the least cost. Finding ways to boost productivity is equally valuable whether in the service of commercial or societal objectives. In short, the principle of value creation should guide the use of resources across all areas of societal concern.

Fortunately, a new type of NGO has emerged that understands the importance of productivity and value creation. Such organizations have often had a remarkable impact. One example is TechnoServe, which has partnered with

which is often best done in conjunction with partners, can allow a company to secure reliable supplies and give suppliers better incentives for quality and efficiency while also substantially improving the incomes and purchasing power of local citizens. A positive cycle of economic and social development results.

both regional and global corporations to promote the development of competitive agricultural clusters in more than 30 countries. Root Capital accomplishes a similar objective by providing financing to farmers and businesses that are too large for microfinance but too small for normal bank financing. Since 2000, Root Capital has lent more than $200 million to 282 businesses, through which it has reached 400,000 farmers and artisans. It has financed the cultivation of 1.4 million acres of organic agriculture in Latin America and Africa. Root Capital regularly works with corporations, utilizing future purchase orders as collateral for its loans to farmers and helping to strengthen corporate supply chains and improve the quality of purchased inputs.

Some private foundations have begun to see the power of working with businesses to create shared value. The Bill & Melinda Gates Foundation, for example, has formed partnerships with leading global corporations to foster agricultural clusters in developing countries. The foundation carefully focuses on commodities where climate and soil conditions give a particular region a true competitive advantage. The partnerships bring in NGOs like TechnoServe and Root Capital, as well as government officials, to work on precompetitive issues that improve the cluster and upgrade the value chain for all participants. This approach recognizes that helping small farmers increase their yields will not create any lasting benefits unless there are ready buyers for their crops, other enterprises that can process the crops once they are harvested, and a local cluster that includes efficient logistical infrastructure, input availability, and the like. The active engagement of corporations is essential to mobilizing these elements.

Forward-thinking foundations can also serve as honest brokers and allay fears by mitigating power imbalances between small local enterprises, NGOs, governments, and companies. Such efforts will require a new assumption that shared value can come only as a result of effective collaboration among all parties.

When a firm builds clusters in its key locations, it also amplifies the connection between its success and its communities' success. A firm's growth has multiplier effects, as jobs are created in supporting industries, new companies are seeded, and demand for ancillary services rises. A company's efforts to improve framework conditions

Government Regulation and Shared Value

THE RIGHT KIND OF GOVERNMENT REGULATION can encourage companies to pursue shared value; the wrong kind works against it and even makes trade-offs between economic and social goals inevitable.

Regulation is necessary for well-functioning markets, something that became abundantly clear during the recent financial crisis. However, the ways in which regulations are designed and implemented determine whether they benefit society or work against it.

Regulations that enhance shared value set goals and stimulate innovation. They highlight a societal objective and create a level playing field to encourage companies to invest in shared value rather than maximize short-term profit. Such regulations have a number of characteristics:

First, they set clear and measurable social goals, whether they involve energy use, health matters, or safety. Where appropriate, they set prices for resources (such as water) that reflect true costs. Second, they set performance standards but do not prescribe the methods to achieve them—those are left to companies. Third, they define phase-in periods for meeting standards, which reflect the investment or new-product cycle in the industry. Phase-in periods give companies time to develop and introduce new products and processes in a way consistent with the economics of their business. Fourth, they put in place universal measurement and performance-reporting systems, with government investing in infrastructure for collecting reliable benchmarking data (such as nutritional deficiencies in each community). This motivates and

---

for the cluster spill over to other participants and the local economy. Workforce development initiatives, for example, increase the supply of skilled employees for many other firms as well.

At Nespresso, Nestlé also worked to build clusters, which made its new procurement practices far more effective. It set out to build agricultural, technical, financial, and logistical firms and capabilities in each coffee region, to further support efficiency and high-quality local production. Nestlé led efforts to increase access to essential agricultural inputs such as plant stock, fertilizers, and irrigation equipment; strengthen regional farmer co-ops by helping them finance shared wet-milling facilities for producing higher-quality beans; and support an extension program to advise all farmers on

enables continual improvement beyond current targets. Finally, appropriate regulations require efficient and timely reporting of results, which can then be audited by the government as necessary, rather than impose detailed and expensive compliance processes on everyone.

Regulation that discourages shared value looks very different. It forces compliance with particular practices, rather than focusing on measurable social improvement. It mandates a particular approach to meeting a standard— blocking innovation and almost always inflicting cost on companies. When governments fall into the trap of this sort of regulation, they undermine the very progress that they seek while triggering fierce resistance from business that slows progress further and blocks shared value that would improve competitiveness.

To be sure, companies locked into the old mindset will resist even well-constructed regulation. As shared value principles become more widely accepted, however, business and government will become more aligned on regulation in many areas. Companies will come to understand that the right kind of regulation can actually foster economic value creation.

Finally, regulation will be needed to limit the pursuit of exploitative, unfair, or deceptive practices in which companies benefit at the expense of society. Strict antitrust policy, for example, is essential to ensure that the benefits of company success flow to customers, suppliers, and workers.

growing techniques. It also worked in partnership with the Rainforest Alliance, a leading international NGO, to teach farmers more-sustainable practices that make production volumes more reliable.

In the process, Nestlé's productivity improved.

A good example of a company working to improve framework conditions in its cluster is Yara, the world's largest mineral fertilizer company. Yara realized that the lack of logistical infrastructure in many parts of Africa was preventing farmers from gaining efficient access to fertilizers and other essential agricultural inputs, and from transporting their crops efficiently to market. Yara is tackling this problem through a $60 million investment in a program to improve ports and roads, which is designed to create agricultural growth corridors in Mozambique and Tanzania. The company is working on this initiative with local governments and support from the Norwegian government. In Mozambique alone, the corridor is expected to benefit more than 200,000 small farmers and create 350,000 new jobs. The improvements will help Yara grow its business but will support the whole agricultural cluster, creating huge multiplier effects.

The benefits of cluster building apply not only in emerging economies but also in advanced countries. North Carolina's Research Triangle is a notable example of public and private collaboration that has created shared value by developing clusters in such areas as information technology and life sciences. That region, which has benefited from continued investment from both the private sector and local government, has experienced huge growth in employment, incomes, and company performance, and has fared better than most during the downturn.

To support cluster development in the communities in which they operate, companies need to identify gaps and deficiencies in areas such as logistics, suppliers, distribution channels, training, market organization, and educational institutions. Then the task is to focus on the weaknesses that represent the greatest constraints to the company's own productivity and growth, and distinguish those areas that the company is best equipped to influence directly from those in which collaboration is more cost-effective. Here is where the shared value opportunities will be greatest. Initiatives that address cluster weaknesses that constrain companies will be much more effective than community-focused corporate social responsibility programs, which often have limited impact because they take on too many areas without focusing on value.

But efforts to enhance infrastructure and institutions in a region often require collective action, as the Nestlé, Yara, and Research Triangle examples show. Companies should try to enlist partners to share the cost, win support, and assemble the right skills. The most successful cluster development programs are ones that involve collaboration within the private sector, as well as trade associations, government agencies, and NGOs.

Creating Shared Value in Practice

Not all profit is equal—an idea that has been lost in the narrow, short-term focus of financial markets and in much management thinking. Profits involving a social purpose represent a higher form of capitalism—one that will enable society to advance more rapidly while allowing companies to grow even more. The result is a positive cycle of company and community prosperity, which leads to profits that endure.

Creating shared value presumes compliance with the law and ethical standards, as well as mitigating any harm caused by the business, but goes far beyond that. The opportunity to create economic value through creating societal value will be one of the most powerful forces driving growth in the global economy. This thinking represents a new way of understanding customers, productivity, and the external influences on corporate success. It highlights the immense human needs to be met, the large new markets to serve, and the internal costs of social and community deficits—as well as the competitive advantages available from addressing them. Until recently, companies have simply not approached their businesses this way.

Creating shared value will be more effective and far more sustainable than the majority of today's corporate efforts in the social arena. Companies will make real strides on the environment, for example, when they treat it as a productivity driver rather than a feel-good response to external pressure. Or consider access to housing. A shared value approach would have led financial services companies to create innovative products that prudently increased access to home ownership. This was recognized by the Mexican construction company Urbi, which pioneered a mortgage-financing "rent-to-own" plan. Major U.S. banks, in contrast, promoted unsustainable financing vehicles that turned out to be socially and economically devastating, while claiming they were socially responsible because they had charitable contribution programs.

How Shared Value Differs from Corporate Social Responsibility

CREATING SHARED VALUE (CSV) should supersede corporate social responsibility (CSR) in guiding the investments of companies in their communities. CSR programs focus mostly on reputation and have only a limited connection to the business, making them hard to justify and maintain in the long run. In contrast, CSV is integral to a company's profitability and competitive position. It leverages the unique resources and expertise of the company to create economic value by creating social value.

CSR	→ CSV
Value: doing good	Value: economic and societal benefits relative to cost
Citizenship, philanthropy, sustainability	Joint company and community value creation
Discretionary or in response to external pressure	Integral to competing
Separate from profit maximization	Integral to profit maximization
Agenda is determined by external reporting and personal preferences	Agenda is company specific and internally generated
Impact limited by corporate footprint and CSR budget	Realigns the entire company budget
Example: Fair trade purchasing	**Example:** Transforming procurement to increase quality and yield

In both cases, compliance with laws and ethical standards and reducing harm from corporate activities are assumed.

Inevitably, the most fertile opportunities for creating shared value will be closely related to a company's particular business, and in areas most important to the business. Here a company can benefit the most economically and hence sustain its commitment over time. Here is also where a company brings the most resources to bear, and where its scale and market presence equip it to have a meaningful impact on a societal problem.

Ironically, many of the shared value pioneers have been those with more-limited resources—social entrepreneurs and companies in developing countries. These outsiders have been able to see the opportunities more clearly. In the process, the distinction between for-profits and nonprofits is blurring.

Shared value is defining a whole new set of best practices that all companies must embrace. It will also become an integral part of strategy. The essence of strategy is choosing a unique positioning and a distinctive value chain to deliver on it. Shared value opens up many new needs to meet, new products to offer, new customers to serve, and new ways to configure the value chain. And the competitive advantages that arise from creating shared value will often be more sustainable than conventional cost and quality improvements. The cycle of imitation and zero-sum competition can be broken.

The opportunities to create shared value are widespread and growing. Not every company will have them in every area, but our experience has been that companies discover more and more opportunities over time as their line operating units grasp this concept. It has taken a decade, but GE's Ecomagination initiative, for example, is now producing a stream of fast-growing products and services across the company.

A shared value lens can be applied to every major company decision. Could our product design incorporate greater social benefits? Are we serving all the communities that would benefit from our products? Do our processes and logistical approaches maximize efficiencies in energy and water use? Could our new plant be constructed in a way that achieves greater community impact? How are gaps in our cluster holding back our efficiency and speed of innovation? How could we enhance our community as a business location? If sites are comparable economically, at which one will the local community benefit the most? If a company can improve societal conditions, it will often improve business conditions and thereby trigger positive feedback loops.

The three avenues for creating shared value are mutually reinforcing. Enhancing the cluster, for example, will enable more local procurement and less dispersed supply chains. New products and services that meet social needs or serve overlooked markets will require new value chain choices in areas such as production, marketing, and distribution. And new value chain configurations will create demand for equipment and technology that save energy, conserve resources, and support employees.

Creating shared value will require concrete and tailored metrics for each business unit in each of the three areas. While some companies have begun to track various social impacts, few have yet tied them to their economic interests at the business level.

Shared value creation will involve new and heightened forms of collaboration. While some shared value opportunities are possible for a company to seize on its own, others will benefit from insights, skills, and resources that cut across profit/nonprofit and private/public boundaries. Here, companies will be less successful if they attempt to tackle societal problems on their own, especially those involving cluster development. Major competitors may also need to work together on precompetitive framework conditions, something that has not been common in reputation-driven CSR initiatives. Successful collaboration will be data driven, clearly linked to defined outcomes, well connected to the goals of all stakeholders, and tracked with clear metrics.

Governments and NGOs can enable and reinforce shared value or work against it. (For more on this topic, see the sidebar "Government Regulation and Shared Value.")

The Next Evolution in Capitalism

Shared value holds the key to unlocking the next wave of business innovation and growth. It will also reconnect company success and community success in ways that have been lost in an age of narrow management approaches, short-term thinking, and deepening divides among society's institutions.

Shared value focuses companies on the right kind of profits—profits that create societal benefits rather than diminish them. Capital markets will undoubtedly continue to pressure companies to generate short-term profits, and some companies will surely continue to reap profits at the expense of societal needs. But such profits will often prove to be short-lived, and far greater opportunities will be missed.

The moment for an expanded view of value creation has come. A host of factors, such as the growing social awareness of employees and citizens and the increased scarcity of natural resources, will drive unprecedented opportunities to create shared value.

We need a more sophisticated form of capitalism, one imbued with a social purpose. But that purpose should arise not out of charity but out of a deeper understanding of competition and economic value creation. This next evolution in the capitalist model recognizes new and better ways to develop products, serve markets, and build productive enterprises.

Creating shared value represents a broader conception of Adam Smith's invisible hand. It opens the doors of the pin factory to a wider set of influences. It is not philanthropy but self-interested behavior to create economic value by creating societal value. If all companies individually pursued shared value connected to their particular businesses, society's overall interests would be served. And companies would acquire legitimacy in the eyes of the communities in which they operated, which would allow democracy to work as governments set policies that fostered and supported business. Survival of the fittest would still prevail, but market competition would benefit society in ways we have lost.

Creating shared value represents a new approach to managing that cuts across disciplines. Because of the traditional divide between economic concerns and social ones, people in the public and private sectors have often followed very different educational and career paths. As a result, few managers have the understanding of social and environmental issues required to move beyond today's CSR approaches, and few social sector leaders have the managerial training and entrepreneurial mindset needed to design and implement shared value models. Most business schools still teach the narrow view of capitalism, even though more and more of their graduates hunger for a greater sense of purpose and a growing number are drawn to social entrepreneurship. The results have been missed opportunity and public cynicism.

Business school curricula will need to broaden in a number of areas. For example, the efficient use and stewardship of all forms of resources will define the next-generation thinking on value chains. Customer behavior and marketing courses will have to move beyond persuasion and demand creation to the study of deeper human needs and how to serve nontraditional customer groups. Clusters, and the broader locational influences on company productivity and innovation, will form a new core discipline in business schools; economic development will no longer be left only to public policy and economics departments. Business and government courses will examine the economic impact of societal factors on enterprises, moving beyond the effects of regulation and macroeconomics. And finance will need to rethink how capital markets can actually support true value creation in companies—their fundamental purpose—not just benefit financial market participants.

There is nothing soft about the concept of shared value. These proposed changes in business school curricula are not qualitative and do not depart from economic value creation. Instead, they represent the next stage in our understanding of markets, competition, and business management.

Not all societal problems can be solved through shared value solutions. But shared value offers corporations the opportunity to utilize their skills, resources, and management capability to lead social progress in ways that even the best-intentioned governmental and social sector organizations can rarely match. In the process, businesses can earn the respect of society again.

Originally published in January–February 2011. Reprint R1101C

How to Lead in the Stakeholder Era

by Hubert Joly

IN JUNE 2020, I TRAVELED BACK TO Minneapolis for my final board meeting as chairman of Best Buy. As I drove down Hennepin Avenue, storefronts were boarded up on each side of the street. The city was still scarred from the riots and protests that followed the killing of George Floyd that May. Around the same time, forest fires were raging across Australia and, once again, in California. A few months earlier, a new virus had been identified, unleashing a pandemic that was spreading across the world.

The past year has heightened a realization that had started to gain ground prior to the devastation of 2020: Business does not exist in a vacuum. Even before the onset of the Covid-19 pandemic, a growing number of business leaders were shifting away from Milton Friedman's assertion that the sole purpose of business is to maximize shareholder returns and embracing the idea that business should serve *all* stakeholders: employees, customers, suppliers, and communities as well as shareholders. Although making money was of course an imperative, many leaders were focusing on *why* they were in business and *who* they were serving.

Then a pandemic turned the world upside down. As so many corporations now struggle to emerge from the health crisis and its economic fallout, will businesses and their leaders abandon principles that serve more than just a share price?

I hope not. Now is not the time to retreat. Instead, it is the time to accelerate. The profound multifaceted crisis we are facing has made it even more obvious that business and society cannot thrive if employees, customers, and communities are not healthy; if our planet is on fire; and if our society is fractured. Doing the same things we have been doing for decades while expecting different results would be, in Einstein's words, the very definition of insanity. What we need today is a refoundation of business and capitalism so that we can build a more sustainable future. It is time for business leaders to embrace a declaration of interdependence that prioritizes the common good and recognizes the humanity of all stakeholders.

I know, based on my own experience and reflections over the past 40 years or so, that shifting a business from maximizing profits to serving employees, customers, suppliers, communities, *and* shareholders is not easy. It requires leadership. In this article, I share the philosophy I have developed throughout my career and that was at the core of the resurgence of Best Buy. Ultimately, it is about much more than piecemeal CSR or ESG. It is about fundamentally redefining your company around purpose and learning how to unleash the best people have to offer. It's about putting purpose and people at the heart of business.

The Purpose of Business Is to Contribute to the Common Good

For business to be part of the solution to our collective challenges, we leaders must see companies not as soulless moneymaking entities but as "human organizations" made of individuals working together in support of a shared goal. This goal must contribute to the common good by making a positive difference in people's lives—what author and consultant Lisa Earle McLeod calls a "noble purpose." In this approach, making money remains an imperative, but profits are not the ultimate objective; rather, they are the outcome of a successful strategy rooted in purpose. This is how Best Buy turned its fortunes around and rebounded to heights that, back in 2012, few would have imagined possible. Best Buy is not an exception.

Idea in Brief

The world is clearly facing crises in health, economics, the environment, and social and geopolitical tensions. More and more leaders realize that business and society cannot thrive if these challenges are not surmounted, and they believe that to do that corporations must serve all their stakeholders—not just their investors—in a harmonious fashion.

To that end, leaders need to evolve how they think about their mission and how they lead. Hubert Joly, the former chairman and CEO of Best Buy, explains that we need leaders who want to pursue a noble purpose, are ready to put people at the center of it, and are dedicated to creating an environment where every employee can blossom. This is how business can be a force for good.

Like-minded companies described as "firms of endearment" have outperformed the S&P 500 14-fold over a period of 15 years. Multiple studies have confirmed that purpose indeed pays.

How do leaders make this vision a reality? First, they help articulate a noble purpose. It can be found at the intersection of what the world needs, what you and your team are passionate about, what the company is good at, and how it can earn a good return on its investments. What did that look like for Best Buy? After much soul-searching and analysis, we eventually decided that the company's purpose was to *enrich our customers' lives through technology* by addressing key human needs in areas such as entertainment, productivity, communication, food, security, and health and wellness. That had a deep meaning for us as human beings, and it made business sense. It was also a much bigger, more inspiring idea than simply being a consumer electronics retailer.

Sometimes a company's stated purpose can feel divorced from its operations—just a fancy way to tell the world who you aspire to be. It needs to be more than that. Take Best Buy's investment in products and services to help aging seniors stay in their homes independently. In working toward its goal to serve 5 million seniors in five years, the company has the potential to significantly accelerate growth. How likely is it that we would have tapped this growing market had our

A Declaration of Interdependence

FOUR GUIDING PRINCIPLES for the next era of capitalism.

1. **Find meaning at a personal level.** Work is a key part of our search for meaning as human beings, a path to our fulfillment, and a means to contributing to the common good. It is incumbent upon each of us to discover who we want to be as human beings and leaders, our purpose in life, and how we want to be remembered, and then to align what we do and how we lead with that vision. It is equally important that we seek to understand what drives the people around us and how that connects with the purpose of the organization.

2. **Define a noble purpose for the company.** The purpose of a business is to make a positive difference in the work, serving all stakeholders—customers, suppliers, the community, and shareholders—in a harmonious fashion. Turning a profit is an imperative and an outcome but not the ultimate goal. Companies must be designed as "human organizations" that are guided by a noble purpose and that put people at the center. This applies not just in good times but also when times get tough.

3. **Unleash human magic.** Leaders must learn to create an environment that enables each person to connect their individual purpose with the purpose of the company. They must foster the development of genuine human connections that make everyone feel that they belong and matter. And leaders must develop an organization that encourages autonomy, supports the development of mastery, and nurtures a growth environment. This is what will create extraordinary outcomes.

4. **Reimagine leadership.** As leaders, we need to follow five Be's:

   - Be clear about our purpose, the purpose of people around us, and how those connect with the purpose of the company.

   - Be clear about our role as a leader. It is not to be the smartest person in the room. It is to create an environment in which others can be successful and flourish.

   - Be clear about whom we serve. If we believe we are serving ourselves, our boss, or the CEO, we probably should not be a leader. As leaders, we must serve people on the front lines and the people around us so that they can be their best.

   - Be driven by values and seek to do what is right. That is foundational.

   - Be authentic. We must be ourselves, and not be afraid to be vulnerable. We must use not only our head but also our heart and our soul. Our ears, our eyes, and our guts. We must be human.

purpose been simply to sell electronics to consumers? Not very. But when your purpose is to enrich lives through technology, that market not only seems possible, it makes total sense.

Leaders must ensure that their company's purpose goes beyond words and becomes the cornerstone of strategy and operations. Once articulated, Best Buy's purpose fundamentally transformed our strategy and how we did business, shifting our playing field from the market of consumer electronics to a much broader environment rich in opportunities, which helped to fuel the company's growth and success.

Unleash Human Magic

A noble purpose must be something every employee can relate to in their day-to-day job. For far too many people, work is viewed as a chore, a curse, a punishment, or a means to an end—something you do to pay the bills, go on vacation, and retire. And too often, this is the reality at organizations that put profit ahead of everything else. Sadly, the result is an uninspired workforce; we see that in study after study, including 2020 research by ADP Research Institute in which only 16% of people globally reported being "fully engaged" at work. This is a tragedy of unfulfilled personal and economic potential. But what if we choose to view work in a radically different light? What if leadership becomes about creating an environment where every employee can blossom and become the best, biggest, most beautiful version of themselves?

Consider this interaction: Jordan was a three-year-old whose favorite T. rex toy broke. His mom brought him to the local Best Buy where Santa Claus had "sourced" the T. rex and explained the situation to two sales associates. These associates could have directed Jordan's mom to the toy shelves and let her find a replacement. Instead, they went above and beyond to "save" the T. rex. Playing doctor, they took the broken dinosaur in for "surgery" behind the counter, discreetly exchanging it for a new one while narrating the lifesaving procedure being performed. After a few minutes, they handed over the "cured" dinosaur to a beaming, excited Jordan.

There aren't standard operating procedures at Best Buy—or a memo from me as leader—detailing how to deal with sick dinosaurs. Instead, this moment was the result of creating an environment that recognizes and values such human creativity. Work for the two employees was not just about collecting a paycheck or selling a new toy. It was about putting a grin back on a little boy's face. Work was for them, in the words of poet Khalil Gibran, love made visible.

How can we as leaders transform companies into places where all employees are willing and able to give their very best, not only to customers but to each other, to suppliers, to their communities, and to shareholders?

The foundation or spark of this magic is to treat work as an essential element of people's humanity and as a way of finding meaning and fulfillment in life. Start by asking yourself and people across your organization, "What drives you?"—a question that I find rarely gets asked in corporate environments. The answer helps people discover a sense of personal purpose, which in turn determines how they relate to their work. When I was at Best Buy, I always found the simplicity and humanity of people's answers striking. Often, managers talk about friends, family, and colleagues—real people who matter to them and motivate them.

One of the most crucial roles for any leader is helping people at all levels of the organization make the connection between what drives them and the company's noble purpose. This may seem like a woolly step. But being able to infuse what we do every day with a bigger sense of *why* we do it helps foster energy, drive, and direction in everyone—from front liners to the CEO. I saw the power of this at one of our stores in Boston, where the store manager asked all employees—every single one—about their dreams in life and then regularly collaborated with them one-on-one toward their goals. Not coincidentally, this store was a top performer. Similarly, during one of our executive team retreats, each of us shared over dinner our life story, what drove us, and how it related to Best Buy's purpose. I remember that this conversation had a profound impact on how we decided to shape the company's purpose and make the company a force for good in the world.

These are not soft practices. The link between personal and collective purpose and how much people are willing and able to invest themselves at work is well-documented. This is the dimension that powers corporations as purposeful human organizations and, when coupled with a sound strategy anchored in a noble purpose, results in extraordinary performance. This is human magic.

So, ask yourself: How can you help connect your team members' search for meaning with the company's noble purpose? A simple way to start is by treating people as individuals who are valued for their unique talents—not as "human capital." This sounds simple and basic, but it has an enormous impact when you actually practice it. I still remember a young employee who explained to me that he felt seen as an individual at Best Buy and what a difference that made to him. He had been hired at 18 years old, shy and unsure of himself. When asked about meaningful experiences at Best Buy, he immediately recounted a visit by his district manager to his store. The manager, who had met him back when he was hired, recognized him and knew his name. That one small moment of connection left a lasting impression. He wasn't just a "Blue Shirt." He was an individual who was known and who mattered. Two years in, the once shy, unsure kid was flourishing and confident.

This is what putting people at the center means. This is the job of the leader in a world driven by more than shareholders. It is the best foundation for learning how to serve all your stakeholders today and in the future.

Purpose and People When Things Get Tough

Putting purpose and people at the center is not a luxury reserved for good times. It is even more crucial for leaders to stay the course during challenging crises like the pandemic, which test the spirit and humanity of purposeful organizations. During my time as CEO of Best Buy, few moments tested us as meaningfully as when Hurricane Maria devastated Puerto Rico in September 2017. The storm knocked out the island's electrical and communications infrastructure. Homes were blown apart or flooded beyond repair. Roads were impassible. Hospitals were inaccessible or evacuated. Best Buy had about 300 employees on the island in our stores and our distribution center. At first, we could not locate any of them.

Our team sprang into action. After we accounted for everyone, we learned that some employees had lost their homes and all their possessions, and many didn't have enough food and clean water. Within a few days, the team organized a cargo plane and arrived in Puerto Rico with the first shipment of emergency supplies. We gave employees cash to buy necessary items and paid them for four weeks after the storm, even though the stores were closed. We also continued to pay any employee who volunteered in the community to help rebuild the island. All told, that cargo plane made 14 trips to Puerto Rico filled with supplies of diapers, water, and food, and made seven trips to bring employees to the mainland. Over time, we helped our people piece their lives back together.

This was in mid-December 2017. If you work in the retail sector, you know what that means: Our stores were closed during key weeks of holiday shopping. But I couldn't have cared less about that. Our employees felt cared for, and we were open for business a mere three months after Maria—a case study in resilience and purpose. And much like we helped our employees, they in turn, helped Best Buy. Within a year, the stores and our distribution facility on the island were open again. Remarkably, our year-on-year sales in each of those locations soared 10% to 15%. But in my mind, our employees' commitment to helping each other through the trauma of losing everything overnight was the real achievement.

Clearly, none of this is easy. Businesses will face obstacles and difficult choices. But, in good times as in challenging ones, it is one of our main responsibilities as leaders to create, nurture, and embody a collective spirit that puts people at the center of everything we do.

The End of Zero-Sum Leadership

Putting people at the center of business means fostering caring and authentic relationships. This should occur within a company but also with all the company's stakeholders—customers, vendors, local communities, and shareholders—in a way that not only contributes to the company's purpose but also creates great outcomes for each of them.

The corporations that will thrive coming out of the pandemic are those that will treat customers as human beings with needs, not walking wallets. They will connect and collaborate with vendors as partners, benefiting both sides and serving customers. They will contribute to their communities in a way that aligns with their noble purpose. They will reject the view of shareholders as soulless and obsessed with short-term profits at all costs. This shift in investor mindset, still in process and led by BlackRock CEO Larry Fink, prioritizes investing in companies that care about their impact on the environment and their communities, and it reinforces the belief that purpose and people (and planet) are at the heart of successful, sustainable business. The companies that will thrive will refuse to see the world as a zero-sum game. They will choose "and" instead of "or." It won't always be easy; there is the temptation to simply "greenwash" and say you're sustainable but not behave as such. Leaders must resist this temptation and serve all stakeholders in word and deed.

It is past time that we as leaders acknowledge that our role has changed in three fundamental ways. One, it is no longer simply about maximizing shareholder value; it is about making a positive difference in the world. Two, the job of leaders is to maximize performance not by choosing among stakeholders but by embracing, mobilizing, and serving all of them in line with a noble purpose, and refusing zero-sum games along the way. Three, the purposeful human organization cannot flourish with the traditional top-down model of the powerful and infallible hero-leader driven by power, fame, glory, or money. What is required now is a leadership approach that puts purpose and people at the heart of business.

This is how, together, we can begin to reinvent capitalism so that it contributes to a more sustainable future.

Originally published on hbr.org, May 13, 2021. Reprint H06CH2

Use Storytelling to Explain Your Company's Purpose

by John Coleman

THE IDEA OF "PURPOSE" HAS swept the corporate world. Encouraged by evangelists such as Simon Sinek, myriad firms like Nike, Adidas, Pepsi, and Coca-Cola are devoting real time and attention to explaining why they do what they do. The idea of purpose was central to a book I coauthored, *Passion and Purpose*.

But activating purpose is impossible without storytelling, at both the corporate and individual levels. As I've written previously, while purpose is essential to a strong corporate culture, it is often activated and reinforced through narrative.[1] Each individual must learn to connect their drive to the organization's purpose and to articulate their story to others.

This is hard for most business leaders. Great leaders are often humble and reticent about themselves. This impulse is admirable, but it falls short of what's needed to inspire people to join in the purpose of an organization. And many businesspeople feel more comfortable with waterfall charts and P&Ls than with telling their own stories. But only narrative can do that. Storytelling is a skill that leaders can—and should—hone.

I learned this lesson, most acutely, from Marshall Ganz, who teaches what he calls "public narrative" at the Harvard Kennedy School of Government. Ganz argues that for people to inspire others with the mission of their organization or cause, they must first link that mission to their own motivations, and then connect it through story to the motivations of the people they hope to persuade. Ganz has developed a simple framework for those who want to develop a narrative approach to their purpose-driven organizations: "Self, Us, Now."[2]

To create a public narrative for your own organization, start with "self." This is perhaps the most difficult part for many businesspeople because it involves focusing on real events in one's own life and explaining how those incidents established the values that later link to the values of the organization.

An excellent example of this is Steve Jobs's address to the Stanford graduating class in 2005. The address was largely a deeply personal reflection on Jobs's own history—his working-class upbringing, his dropping out of college. Perhaps more important, however, he spoke about how his love of calligraphy instilled in him a love of design that would later guide his work at Apple, and how his cancer diagnosis reinforced his deep desire to live passionately and authentically—as if each day were his last. It's beautiful storytelling, and it gives you a glimpse into who Jobs was, what he valued, and how that later guided his work at Apple and elsewhere. What's compelling about Jobs's address is that it seems authentic and raw. A great story of self has to be a *real* story of self. Finding that story may require a leader to reflect deeply on her past and motivations, and communicate them honestly—even those parts that are embarrassing or imperfect.

The next step, "us," aims to connect those values with broader shared values of the audience—clients or employees, for example. In this step, you weave your own personal narrative into the narratives of others through shared values, experiences, hopes, and aspirations. In doing so you create a common narrative for the group or organization. In literature, a well-known example of this (one that Ganz often highlights in class) is the St. Crispin's Day speech from William Shakespeare's *Henry V*. In it, King Henry, attempting to motivate an English army demoralized by their lack of strength, calls on his troops to be a "band of brothers" fighting valiantly together for each other, their country, and the values they share.

Idea in Brief

Activating purpose is impossible without storytelling, at both the corporate and individual levels. But telling a story that will inspire people to connect with your organization's reason for being is a skill that doesn't come naturally to many business leaders. Author John Coleman offers examples of compelling narratives and explains how anyone can use Marshall Ganz's "Self, Us, Now" framework to tell a persuasive story about organizational purpose.

While it's miles away from the battlefield of Agincourt, Burt's Bees is a good example of how a business has applied this technique. They feature the story of their founder, Burt Shavitz, on their website, documenting how the story of Burt and his partner, Roxanne, became "our story," the story of the company and its clients. Before his death, Burt himself was a company spokesperson for years beyond his operational involvement. A great "story of us" establishes a community and its values, and how they came to be.

Finally, the close is what Ganz calls the "now"—an urgent call to action for those who wish to share the purpose of a group or an organization. Consider St. Jude Children's Research Hospital. The organization's purpose is "Finding cures. Saving children," and their site is filled with the stories of the kids they serve. Their call to action—often, simply to give financially—is simple, direct, and compelling in their videos and materials.

Kickstarter, similarly, had an impactful way of asking people to join its team in its early years. The narrative began with its founder telling the story of the company (the "self"). Their website included pictures and short descriptions of each and every company employee ("the us"). Finally, the narrative culminated its "now" call to action with a Careers page proclaiming: "Love Kickstarter? You'll fit right in." Stories like these are most powerful when they are individually authentic, build to a collective narrative and values, and then seal the deal by asking the person reading, watching, or listening to join in.

Storytelling can be awkward and unfamiliar for many professionals, particularly if you're sharing personal experiences. Yet the motivation for this storytelling is not self-aggrandizement but to create a purpose and culture that others can share. Purpose is what builds real passion, motivation, and buy-in for the stakeholders of any organization. And it can be articulated by leaders who've learned to tell their stories and the stories of the organizations, people, and causes they serve.

Adapted from content posted on hbr.org, November 24, 2015. Reprint H02IEP

Notes

1. John Coleman, "Six Components of a Great Corporate Culture," hbr.org, May 6, 2013, https://hbr.org/2013/05/six-components-of-culture.

2. Serena Zhang and Voop de Vulpillieres, "Public Narrative Participant Guide," adapted from the works Marshall Ganz, Harvard University, 2021, https://www.ndi.org/sites/default/files/Public%20Narrative%20Participant%20Guide.pdf.

About the Contributors

JULIE BATTILANA is the Joseph C. Wilson Professor of Business Administration in the Organizational Behavior unit at Harvard Business School and the Alan L. Gleitsman Professor of Social Innovation at Harvard Kennedy School.

SUNDAR BHARADWAJ is the Coca-Cola Company Chair of Marketing and a professor at the University of Georgia's Terry College of Business.

IVY BUCHE is the Associate Director of Business Transformation Initiative at IMD in Lausanne, Switzerland.

AARON K. CHATTERJI is the Mark Burgess & Lisa Benson-Burgess Distinguished Professor of Business and Public Policy at Duke University's Fuqua School of Business and a professor of business administration at Duke's Sanford School of Public Policy.

JOHN COLEMAN is the author of the *HBR Guide to Crafting Your Purpose* (Harvard Business Review Press, 2022).

NICK CRAIG is the president and founder of the Core Leadership Institute.

CHARLES DHANARAJ is the J. Mack Robinson Professor of International Business and the academic director of the DBA program at Robinson College of Business at Georgia State University. He was formerly a professor of strategy at Temple University's Fox School of Business, where he was also the founding executive director of the Translational Research Center.

ADAM M. GRANT is an organizational psychologist at Wharton, the author of *Think Again,* and the host of the podcast *WorkLife with Adam Grant.*

HANNAH GROVE is the former global chief marketing officer of State Street and a nonexecutive director of the investment firm abrdn.

RANJAY GULATI is the Paul R. Lawrence MBA Class of 1942 Professor of Business Administration at Harvard Business School. He is the author of *Deep Purpose*.

B. TOM HUNSAKER is the associate dean of innovation and academic director of Thunderbird Applied Learning at the Thunderbird School of Global Management at Arizona State University.

ALISON JAMES is the former global CHRO of BIC and the current executive director of the BIC Corporate Foundation.

HUBERT JOLY is the former chairman and CEO of Best Buy, a senior lecturer of business administration at Harvard Business School, and the author of *The Heart of Business* (Harvard Business Review Press, 2021).

MARISSA KIMSEY is a doctoral student in management at the University of Oxford's Saïd Business School.

JONATHAN KNOWLES is the founder of the strategic advisory firm Type 2 Consulting.

MARK R. KRAMER cofounded FSG, a global social impact consulting firm, with Michael Porter and is a senior adviser and its board chair. He is also a senior fellow at the Harvard Kennedy School of Government.

THOMAS W. MALNIGHT is a professor emeritus of strategy and management and the former faculty director of the Business Transformation Initiative at IMD in Lausanne, Switzerland. He is a coauthor of *Ready? The 3Rs of Preparing Your Organization for the Future.*

ANNE-CLAIRE PACHE is the Chaired Professor in Social Innovation at ESSEC Business School.

MICHAEL E. PORTER is the Bishop William Lawrence University Professor, Emeritus, at Harvard Business School. He is a frequent contributor to *Harvard Business Review* and a seven-time McKinsey Award winner.

ROBERT E. QUINN is a professor emeritus of management and organizations at the University of Michigan's Ross School of Business and a cofounder of the school's Center for Positive Organizations.

OMAR RODRÍGUEZ-VILÁ is Professor in the Practice of Marketing and the academic director of education at the Business & Society Institute at Emory University's Goizueta Business School.

METIN SENGUL is a professor of management at the University of Texas at Austin's McCombs School of Business.

SCOTT SNOOK is an executive fellow at Harvard Business School. He served in the US Army Corps of Engineers for more than 22 years.

ANJAN V. THAKOR is the John E. Simon Professor of Finance and the director of doctoral programs at the Olin Business School at Washington University in St. Louis.

MICHAEL W. TOFFEL is the Senator John Heinz Professor of Environmental Management at Harvard Business School.

Index

Engage with HBR content the way you want, on any device.

With HBR's subscription plans, you can access world-renowned case studies from Harvard Business School and receive four **free eBooks**. Download and customize prebuilt **slide decks and graphics** from our **Data & Visuals** collection. With HBR's archive, top 50 best-selling articles, and five new articles every day, HBR is more than just a magazine.

Subscribe Today
HBR.org/success